D0102412

EALING AND HANWELL PAST

First published 1991
by Historical Publications Ltd
32 Ellington Street, London N7 8PL
(Telephone 071–607 1628)

© **Peter Hounsell 1991**

All rights reserved
Unauthorised duplication
contravenes applicable laws

ISBN 0 948667 13 3

Typeset by Historical Publications Ltd
and Fakenham Photosetting
Printed and bound in Great Britain by
Biddles Ltd, Guildford and King's Lynn

EALING AND HANWELL PAST

A Visual History
of Ealing and Hanwell

by
Peter Hounsell

P. Hounsell
29-XI-91

HISTORICAL PUBLICATIONS

Acknowledgements

I should like to thank my colleagues Maureen Gooding and Ann Terre, the staff of the Local History Library in Ealing, for allowing me generous access to the collections, and for supplying the majority of the illustrations. The staff at the Guildhall Library and Gunnersbury Museum have also been most helpful.

The Illustrations

Almost all of the illustrations are reproduced by kind permission of the London Borough of Ealing Library and Information Service. We are most grateful for their generous co-operation. The Gunnersbury Park Museum supplied Illustrations *14 and 62*, and also *61* with the permission of M.J. Fenton.

The jacket illustration is of *Ealing Haven Station* (now Ealing Broadway), *c*1840. From a watercolour by an unknown artist

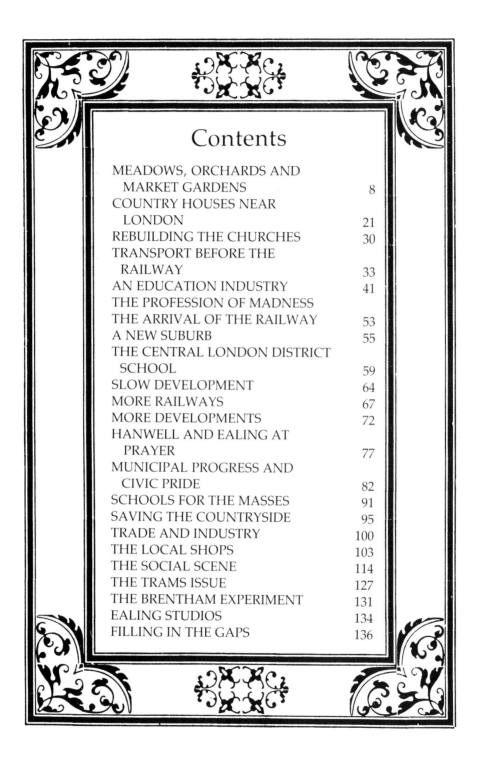

Contents

Further Reading

Both Ealing and Hanwell are short of good modern histories. In the absence of a replacement for C.M. Neaves' *History of Greater Ealing*, originally published in 1930, Kate McEwan provides a lively topographical introduction to the whole borough in *Ealing Walkabout* (1984). More dedicated researchers will turn to the *Victoria County History of Middlesex*: Hanwell is included in Volume III (1962) whilst Ealing is in Volume VII (1982). My own debt to the work of Michael Jahn is considerable; a condensed version of his thesis is found in 'Suburban development in outer West London 1850–1900', published in *The Rise of Suburbia*, edited by F.M.L. Thompson (1982).

The best-known older histories are Edith Jackson *The Annals of Ealing* (1898), T. Faulkner *The History and Antiquities of Brentford, Ealing and Chiswick* (1845) and Montagu Sharpe *Some account of bygone Hanwell and its chapelry of New Brentford* (1924). Charles Jones wrote two volumes of reminiscences: *Ealing: from Village to Corporate Town* (1902), and its continuation, *A Decade of Progress 1901–1911* (1911).

On particular topics, Susan Stewart has written a useful pamphlet on the Central London District School (n.d.) and the Brentham Society one on *Brentham: Ealing's Garden Suburb* (1977).

Other photographs from Ealing's Local History collection will be found in *Ealing as it was* (1980), *Ealing in the 1930s and 1940s* (1985) and *Environs of Ealing in old photographs* (1984).

Introduction

The scope of this visual history is the Borough of Ealing, formed in 1901, and the adjacent parish of Hanwell. Both are now part of the much larger London Borough of Ealing which also embraces the old boroughs of Acton and Southall. If the coverage of the two areas is unequal it reflects their relative sizes.

Ealing is often referred to as the 'Queen of the Suburbs', an epithet bestowed at the end of the nineteenth century. Some residents still think of it in these terms, although the golden age has surely long since passed away. Nevertheless, streets in central Ealing still retain much of their Victorian character, with handsome villas and established trees. In recent years a strong determination to resist intrusive development and to preserve the environment has emerged.

There have, of course, been numerous changes. Many of the larger houses were divided into flats, and some were demolished to make way for estates. The shopping centre has been transformed by the building of new shopping malls, and many artisans' dwellings have been swept away by redevelopment. Offices have replaced houses along the Uxbridge Road.

Hanwell has been a victim to its proximity to Ealing, and its shops have struggled to survive. The long thin shape of the parish has always worked to its disadvantage. However, Hanwell has its loyal supporters who preserve a spirit of independence.

Although this book is not designed as a student text I have been conscious of the lack of a suitable introduction to the history of the area. The content is necessarily selective but I hope that the book will provide at least a starting point for more detailed research.

Peter Hounsell

1. *A View of Ealing* by Chatelain, 1750. There is some doubt as to whether the view is of Ealing at all since neither the architecture of the church (see illustration 26) nor the surrounding buildings seem to have much relationship to what is known of the period.

Meadows, Orchards and Market Gardens

ORIGINS

The centre of Ealing is only 5½ miles from Hyde Park Corner, but until the latter part of the nineteenth century the parishes of Ealing and its westerly neighbour Hanwell were still largely rural. But the rapid pace of suburban development from the 1880s through to the 1930s obliterated that rural world, traces of which survive only in parks and other open spaces. There are regrettably few early illustrations to show us what that vanished world was like.

The historic parishes of Ealing and Hanwell were both originally larger than the districts that bear these names today. The southern boundary of both was the River Thames at Brentford, the part known as Old Brentford being in Ealing parish, that known as New Brentford in Hanwell. The northern boundary was that much less illustrious river, the Brent, whose course also formed Hanwell's western boundary. The ground rises in a gentle slope from the Thames to the pronounced ridge at Hanger Hill, Castle Hill and Cuckoo Hill, and then drops more steeply down to the Brent valley.

This geography is reflected in the soils of the area, with a mixture of gravels and brick-earth near the Thames and London clay on the higher ground to the north. This had implications for the way the area was settled and how the land was used.

Evidence of human occupation of the area from early times exists both in the archaeological record and later from place names. Archaeological finds have been concentrated near the River Thames,

2. *Old Brentford*, then part of the parish of Ealing, in 1821.

consistent with Brentford's importance as a crossing point, but there are scattered finds, from the neolithic period onwards, throughout the area. The names in both areas are predominately Anglo-Saxon: 'Ealing' derives from 'Gillingas', meaning the people of gilla, and there have been many variants of the name, for example Yeling, Zelling, Eling, before the nineteenth century.'Hanwell' is seemingly a combination of the words 'hana' (a cock) and 'weille' (a spring or stream). The element 'Hangra', which appears in Hanger Hill and Pits-hanger, denotes a wooded slope.

Domesday Book, the great survey of the wealth of England commissioned by William I, and produced in 1086, is often regarded as the starting point for the local history of an area. However, the Domesday evidence in this case is confusing. The manor of Hanwell is recorded as one of the properties of Westminster Abbey, to whom it had been given in the tenth century; Ealing, on the other hand, is not identified by name at all and is thought to be contained within the Bishop of London's extensive manor of Fulham, as is Ealing's easterly neighbour Acton. By the thirteenth century Hanwell manor

had been absorbed into that of its northerly neighbour Greenford, and many aspects of its development were linked more closely with Greenford than Ealing.

The unique census of Ealing in 1599 records 426 people in 85 households. Thirty-nine heads of household were described as *husbandmen*; Ealing was clearly a largely agricultural place, but significantly there were already city businessmen with estates in Ealing, a tendency that was to grow in the following two centuries.

In 1664 the population of Ealing was 116 households, with a further 259 in Old Brentford. In Hanwell, by contrast, geographically much smaller, there were only 73 households, with a further 136 in New Brentford. Brentford, strategically placed by the Thames, was growing much faster than the rest of the two parishes and becoming an important commercial and industrial centre.

3. *Hanwell in the late eighteenth century*. A view from the Uxbridge Road looking east, with the Brent Bridge in the centre.

4. *Ealing in 1823* (precise location unknown).

5. *Ealing in 1823* (precise location unknown).

6. *Hanwell Church and Rectory* overlooking the River Brent in 1793.

FOOD FOR LONDON

The more northerly parts of the area were given over to agriculture, with the houses clustered around the churches, and beside the Uxbridge Road. But these were not isolated rural areas: only a few miles from the centre of London they were necessarily caught up in the growth of the metropolitan area. Indeed, the presence of such a large market dictated the progress of agriculture in much of West Middlesex. This worked in two directions: the transfer of arable land to grass, to produce hay for the animals in the city, and the establishment of market gardens to produce fruit and vegetables.

Rocque's map of 1746, whilst not topographically exact, gives a clear impression of the pattern of land use in mid-century, and the location of the houses. The development of Brentford as an urban centre is evident and the concentration of small plots of land just to the north of the built-up area – the market gardens – was determined both by the lighter soils near the river and the better transport facilities. Further north the regular pattern of enclosed arable fields is contrasted with the waste, such as Ealing and Hanwell commons, and the meadows, particularly near the River Brent, which regularly inundated them.

The move away from arable farming was a gradual one. In 1803 about half the acreage in Hanwell was under grass. In Ealing in 1799, 1377 acres were producing grass, as against 1027 acres of arable and 289 acres of market gardens. When Ealing was surveyed in 1840 under the terms of the Tithe Commutation Act of 1838 there were only 834 acres of arable land left but some 1978 acres of meadow and pasture. The amount of land used for market gardens had increased to 467 acres, comprising some 36 separate gardens. In Hanwell in 1842 there were some 789 acres of meadow and pasture whilst arable land had diminished to a mere 200 acres. By the 1840s most of the remaining common land had been enclosed, in Hanwell's case finally by an Act of Parliament in 1814, in Ealing's by a long process of conversion without legislation. There were a number of orchards, with lower growing fruit bushes and strawberries growing beneath the fruit trees.

Both areas were able to draw on abundant supplies of manure, drawn from the stables of London. By the 1840s there were only two farms in Hanwell, Cuckoo Farm to the north, and Park Farm. In Ealing the farms and market gardens numbered 50, of which five were over 100 acres in extent, the largest holding being 457 acres. An investigation in 1843 reported that 'the farmhouses attached to the larger estates are of a superior kind, indicating the easy circumstances of the tenants, and a considerable degree of comfort and respectability'.

7. *Ealing Common* in the early nineteenth century.

8. *The River Brent and the Ruislip Road* looking east *c*1910. Greenford is on the left bank, Ealing on the right of the river, and to the right of the road is Brentside farm.

9. Ealing and Hanwell in the 1740s, part of *An Exact Survey of the Cities of London, Westminster, and the Borough of Southwark, and the country near ten miles around*, by John Rocque, published in 1746.

RUSTIC PLEASURES

The entertainments of the population were in keeping with the character of the neighbourhood. In May 1774 John Yeoman 'took a walk up to Ealing to see a grand cricket match, eleven a side Southall and Norwood people against Ealing. It is the same as the children play in our country [Yeoman came from Somerset] only they play to the truth of the play.' Pigeon shooting seems to have been popular in the 1790s and the Old Hats public house was a well-known rendezvous.

The Ealing Fair, held on the village green on the 24th to 26th June, drew people from some distance. On 24 June 1822 William Cobbett, coming into London from the west met 'in all the various modes of conveyance, the cockneys going to Ealing Fair'. Sideshows, amusements and caravans crowded the Green and pony races took place at Ealing Dean. The fair continued to be held until 1880 when, with the changed character of the neighbourhood and complaints about the evils it encouraged, the local council had it suppressed.

Ealing Races,

HELD ON

EALING DEAN,

On the 25th and 26th June, 1818.

Thursday, the First Day.

THE LADIES' CUP,

Value 50 Guineas,

To be run for, by Ponies, not exceeding 13 Hands high, the best of Heats, without Limitation of Weight.

A PRIZE FOR THE SECOND PONY,

Likewise on the same Day, to be run for

Another Silver Cup, No. 1,

Value 50 Guineas,

By Ponies not exceeding 13 Hands, 2 Inches high, the best of Heats, to carry 7 Stone, 7 lb. and 7 lb. allowed for every Inch under.

Friday, the Second Day.

THE WATERLOO CUP,

Value 50 Guineas,

To be run for, by Ponies not exceeding 13 Hands, 1 Inch high, the best of Heats ; 13 Hands, 1 Inch, to carry 7 Stone, and to be allowed 7 lb. for every Inch under.

☞ *The Winner of the Ladies' Cup to carry 7lb. EXTRA.*

A PRIZE FOR THE SECOND PONY,

Likewise to be run for,

Another Silver Cup, No. 2,

Value 50 Pounds,

By Ponies not exceeding 12 Hands high, the best of Heats, without Limitation of Weight.

To start precisely at Twelve o'Clock on each Day.   No Race on any Account after Four o'Clock.

The Ponies to be entered at the Red Lion Inn, *Old Brentford*, on Wednesday, June 17, from 10 o'Clock in the Forenoon until 8 in the Evening, when the Colours of the Riders must be named, and no Pony can possibly be entered after that Day.

N.B. The Prizes may be seen at the Red Lion, and will be delivered on the above Days.

☞ *No Suttling Booths allowed on the Common on any Pretence.*

10. *Ealing Fair* on Ealing Green, a photograph taken in the 1860s. The Queen Victoria public house and the Grove are in the background.

11. *Poster advertising Ealing Races* in June 1818, held on Ealing Dean Common whilst the Fair was held on Ealing Green.

12. *Gunnersbury House c*1750, from an engraving by Chatelain.

Country Houses near London

Proximity to London combined with genteel rusticity made Ealing and Hanwell convenient places for city businessmen and others involved in public affairs to have country houses. Even before the age of mechanised transport the journey from the City or Westminster was not difficult.

In April 1774 John Yeoman, a visitor to London, took a walk from Brentford to Ealing; he commented that 'in the course of that walk, about 2 miles, we went by 5 Esquires seats, one Bishop, one Dukes, and the Princess Amelia House. So I leave the reader to judge the pleasantness of our walk, &, where there was no Gentleman seat, it was gardener's gardens with fruit trees all in full bloom, which makes it like the seat of Paradise.'

Whilst there were a number of such substantial houses with modest gardens, none of these was on the scale of the great landed estates like, for example, the neighbouring Osterley Park.

The major estate was Gunnersbury Park. There had been an estate at Gunnersbury in the Middle Ages, but a new house had been built for Sir John Maynard, MP, lawyer and counsel to Charles II. He employed John Webb, a pupil of Inigo Jones, to build him a Palladian style house, and this was completed in 1663. Defoe praised both the house and its situation: 'from the portico in the back front of the house, you have an exceeding fine prospect of the county of Surrey, the River of Thames, and all the meadows on the borders for some miles, as also a good prospect of London, in clear weather'. The house was occupied from 1763 to 1786 by the Princess Amelia, the youngest daughter of George II, who entertained extensively and held court to a large circle of friends, including the celebrated writer Horace Walpole.

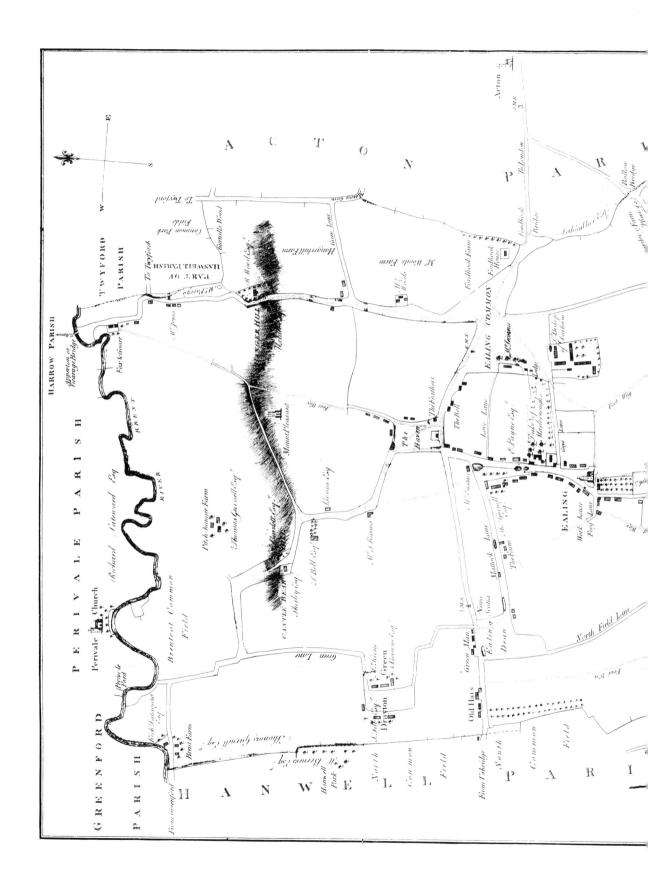

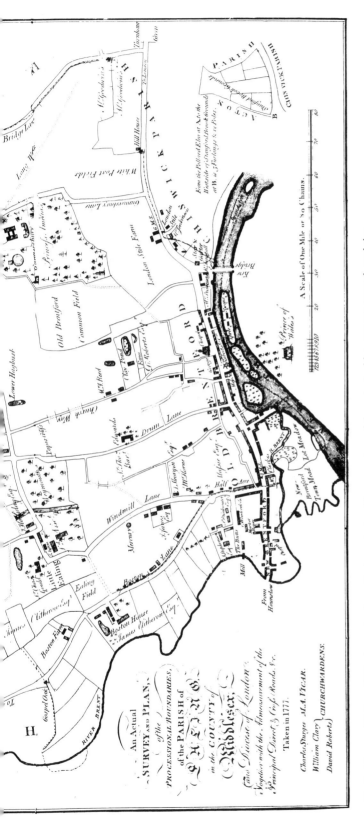

13. *Parish map of Ealing, 1777, drawn to show the boundaries. The occupiers of the principal houses are named, and the contrast between the density of population in Brentford and North Ealing is evident.*

After Princess Amelia's death the estate passed through several hands and after the house was demolished in 1801 the estate was divided into two, with separate owners. A new house was built on each part, known respectively as Gunnersbury House and Gunnersbury Park. Nathan Meyer de Rothschild bought the latter in 1836 and the Rothschild family reunited the old estate in 1889 by acquiring the other house and grounds. Part of the unified estate was sold for building but the two houses, which are very close to each other, were sold to Ealing and Acton councils in 1925 to form a museum and public park operated jointly by the London Boroughs of Ealing and Hounslow.

The oldest surviving house in Ealing is Rochester House in Little Ealing Lane. Little Ealing was a hamlet south west of the main village. The house was built in the early eighteenth century for John Pearce, a London distiller, whose son Zachary became Bishop of Rochester. In 1812 it was occupied by General Dumouriez, a French soldier and politician in exile, and for much of the nineteenth century it was used as a school.

Other eighteenth century houses survive, though most of the larger ones have long since been demolished. Pitshanger Manor, on Ealing Green, now a museum after many years as a public library, was built in the early nineteenth century by Sir John Soane, for his own use. It occupied the site of an earlier house owned by the Gurnell family, who were Quakers with interests in trade and banking. Jonathan Gurnell married into the Wilmer family and acquired a house on Ealing Green; his son Thomas engaged the celebrated architect George Dance the Younger to make additions to the house, in the form of two principal reception rooms, and these were retained when Soane demolished the remainder of the building. During much of the nineteenth century the house was occupied by the Misses Perceval, the daughters of Spencer Perceval, the prime minister, but it was owned by Spencer Walpole, MP and government minister, who had married one of the sisters, and who himself lived in the house next door, The Hall.

Spencer Perceval, known as the Evangelical Prime Minister, lived from 1809 until his assassina-

14. *Gunnersbury Park* in the nineteenth century. It is the larger of the two houses.

15. *Sir John Soane.*

16. *Spencer Perceval.*

tion in 1812, at Elm Grove, a house near Ealing Common. This house, also known as Hickes-on-the-Heath, had had many owners in the preceding century, including John Egerton, Bishop of Durham, and Lord Kinnaird. Although there are many illustrations of the house its building history is unclear. Like Rochester House it was later to house a number of institutions before its demolition at the end of the nineteenth century.

Place House, near Rochester House in Little Ealing, enjoyed a number of aristocratic owners including Earl Brooke and Lord John Manners, whose tenant in 1777 was Thomas Thynne, Viscount Weymouth. Many of these tenancies were short-lived, perhaps reflecting the changing political fortunes of their residents. A later owner of the house, by then known as Ealing Park, was William Lawrence (1783–1867), the distinguished surgeon, whose wife Louisa laid out the gardens, which were highly regarded and visited by Queen Victoria. Her earlier garden at Drayton Villa was illustrated by Loudon. The house still survives, having been used as a school and a convent.

17. *Pitshanger Manor* as rebuilt by John Soane *c*1810. The left wing is all that remains of the earlier house.

18. *Castle Hill Lodge* at the time it was owned by the Duke of Kent. An illustration in *The Beauties of England and Wales* by J.N. Brewer, published in 1816.

There were a number of houses on Castlebar Hill, whose similar names cause much confusion. At the top of Castlebar Road, on the ridge overlooking the Brent Valley, was Castlehill Lodge. This house, with 27 acres of grounds, was bought in 1773 by Francis Burdett, whose son, later Sir Francis Burdett Bt, a famous radical politician, was brought up there. In the 1790s the house began its curious association with the royal family, when Mrs Maria Fitzherbert, the morganatic wife of George, Prince of Wales, moved there. She sold it in 1801 to George's brother, the Duke of Kent, Queen Victoria's father, who installed his mistress there. He employed James Wyatt to improve the house which, as an observer noted 'though not of the first class of noble mansions, is now sufficiently capacious for the accommodation of a large establishment. The building is of rather low, but pleasing proportions. The chief front stands towards the north and has in the centre a portico, with four Ionic columns, surmounted by a triangular pediment, the tympanum being vacant. The hill on which the structure is placed descends from this front with a gentle sweep, and a prospect of some extent is obtained over a tract of country which is of an agreeable though not eminently picturesque character.' Despite the likelihood of Victoria never having been at Castlehill the area surrounding the house has traded on its supposed royal associations in street names such as Victoria Road and Queen's Walk.

Amongst a number of other country houses, including Drayton House, Castlebar Park, and Hanger Hill House, Fordhook, close to the Acton boundary, had interesting literary connections. Henry Fielding, the novelist, was an occupant of the house briefly in the 1750s and gives in a journal entry for May 1754 some of the reasons why people were attracted to Ealing: 'I resolved therefore to visit a little house of mine in the county of Middlesex, in the best air, I believe, in the whole kingdom, and far superior to that of Kensington Gravel Pits [i.e. Notting Hill]; for the gravel is here much wider and deeper and placed higher and more open towards the south, whilst it is guarded from the north by a ridge of hills, and from the smells and smoke of London by its distance, which last is not the fate of Kensington when the wind blows from any corner of the east.' (*Journey of a Voyage to Lisbon*). A later resident of the house was Lady Byron, the widow of the poet.

CASTLE BEAR HILL.

Particulars

OF THE

FREEHOLD AND COPYHOLD

LANDS,

AND OF THE

BUILDING MATERIALS

OF THE FREEHOLD MANSION HOUSE AND OFFICES THEREON,

Late the Property of His Royal Highness the Duke of Kent, deceased,

SITUATE

AT CASTLE BEAR HILL, EALING, MIDDLESEX,

WHICH WILL BE

Peremptorily Sold by Auction,

UPON THE PREMISES,

Pursuant to an Order of the High Court of Chancery made in a Cause FOURNIER against Her Royal Highness the Duchess of Kent, and others.

BY

Mr. WILLIAM STEVENS,

With the approbation of JAMES TROWER, Esq., one of the Masters of the said Court;

THE LANDS

On THURSDAY the 6th Day of AUGUST next,

BETWEEN THE HOURS OF ELEVEN AND TWELVE O'CLOCK IN THE FORENOON,

IN THE TWO FOLLOWING LOTS,

AND THE

BUILDING MATERIALS OF THE MANSION HOUSE AND OFFICES.

ON THE TWO FOLLOWING DAYS,

In Lots, according to the printed Catalogue and Conditions delivered with this Particular.

THE SALE EACH DAY TO COMMENCE AT ELEVEN O'CLOCK IN THE FORENOON.

Printed Particulars and Conditions of Sale may be had (*gratis*) and Catalogues at one shilling each, to be returned to Purchasers, at the said Master's Chambers; of Messrs. Swain, Stevens, Maples, Pearse, and Hunt, Solicitors, Frederick's Place, Old Jewry; of Messrs. Karslake, and Crealock, Solicitors, No. 4, Regent Street, Waterloo Place; and of Messrs. Stevens, and Brenchley, Auctioneers, &c. 36, Old Jewry, of whom may be had Tickets to view the Premises.

19. Sale Catalogue of the Duke of Kent's estate at Castle Hill, 1820s.

20. *Fordhook House c*1810.

21. *Fordhook House* about a hundred years later, somewhat altered.

22. *Hanwell Park*, the garden front, *c*1840.

Boston Manor, unlike most of the houses in the district was owned by one family for over two hundred years. The Clitherow family acquired the estate in 1670 and it passed through the family line until it was sold in 1923. Much of the land was then built over but the house and 20 acres of grounds were preserved as a public amenity. In Hanwell most of the houses were clustered around the church, which stood on high ground overlooking the River Brent. Hanwell, being a much smaller parish than Ealing, had fewer landed estates. Hanwell Park, north of the village, was a considerable estate of 286 acres, with pleasure grounds to the north, whose distinctive avenue of trees is visible on Rocque's map. In 1775 the owners obtained a private Act of Parliament that enabled them to exchange lands with those of Hobbayne's charity, and thus improve their southern aspect. The house was the largest in the parish, with two wings and a portico. After the death of Lord Berners in 1782 the estate was broken up. From the division two other estates emerged: Brent Lodge was acquired by the Rector of Hanwell, G.H. Glasse, in 1795 and formed part of the estate he built up for himself near the church; it was later occupied by Montague Sharpe, the local historian, and finally demolished in the 1930s. The other estate was Hanwell Grove, or the Grove, where Grove Avenue is today.

23. *Brent Lodge*, Hanwell, from the croquet lawn, at the end of the nineteenth century.

Rebuilding the Churches

The medieval church of St Mary, Hanwell was similar in size and style to those of the neighbouring parishes of Greenford, Northolt and Perivale. Although an illustration of the exterior survives, little is known about it. By the 1780s Hanwell's population had grown to a point where this little church was inadequate, whilst the other churches mentioned continued to meet the needs of their parishes up to the twentieth century and still survive.

St Mary's was demolished in 1781 to make way for a new building, designed by Thomas Hardwick, who had already built the chapel at New Brentford, St Lawrence. The incumbent at Hanwell was Samuel Glasse, a chaplain to George III, who made a large contribution to the cost of the new building. He resigned the living in 1785 in favour of his son, George Henry Glasse, a notable classical scholar and schoolmaster. The new church was a simple, classical building with a gallery in the nave and round-headed windows under a cornice and parapet. The exterior was brick, the roof slate, surmounted by a turret with cupola at the west end. It enjoyed a picturesque position overlooking the river.

In Ealing the medieval church of St Mary, of which no pictorial record is thought to survive, had been in a poor structural state throughout the early years of the eighteenth century. In 1718 it was necessary to repair the steeple but the following year the steeple and tower were demolished. The churchwardens were then 'empowered to sell and dispose of all lead and all the ironwork which belonged to the steeple and tower of our parish church lately taken down to the best and most benefit and advantage which can be got from the same and to account for such money arising from the same.'

The remainder of the church collapsed in 1729 although it had not been in used since 1725. In the interim worship had been taking place in a 'slight timber tabernacle'. At a vestry meeting in 1731 it was agreed to obtain estimates to build a new church and start a subscription list to raise the finance to pay for it.

The first stone of the new church was laid in 1735

24. The small medieval church of *St Mary, Hanwell, c1750.*

25. *St Mary's Church, Hanwell*, in 1809.

and the shell was erected at a cost of £1,500. But there were insufficient funds to complete the fittings, which would cost another £1,500. Despite the presence of many wealthy residents in the area it was necessary to obtain a private Act of Parliament, which enabled the parish to raise additional funds from the ratepayers.

But it was not until 1789 that the accounts could finally be wound up, whilst the church had been opened on Trinity Sunday, 1740. The new building was a solid classical edifice, but with little character. Inside, there were galleries, with parts set aside for the pupils of the local private academies, including the nearby Great Ealing School.

Of the many monuments in the church some came from the medieval building. The oldest is that to Richard Amandesham, a 'mercer and merchant of the staple of Calys', *c*1490. A prime minister, Spencer Perceval, a home secretary, Spencer Walpole, and several MPs are commemorated, alongside the radical politician John Horne Tooke (1736–1812), whose memorial was provided in 1919 by the New England Society of New York in recognition of his support during the American War of Independence.

26. *St Mary's Church, Ealing*. The eighteenth century church as depicted about 1800.

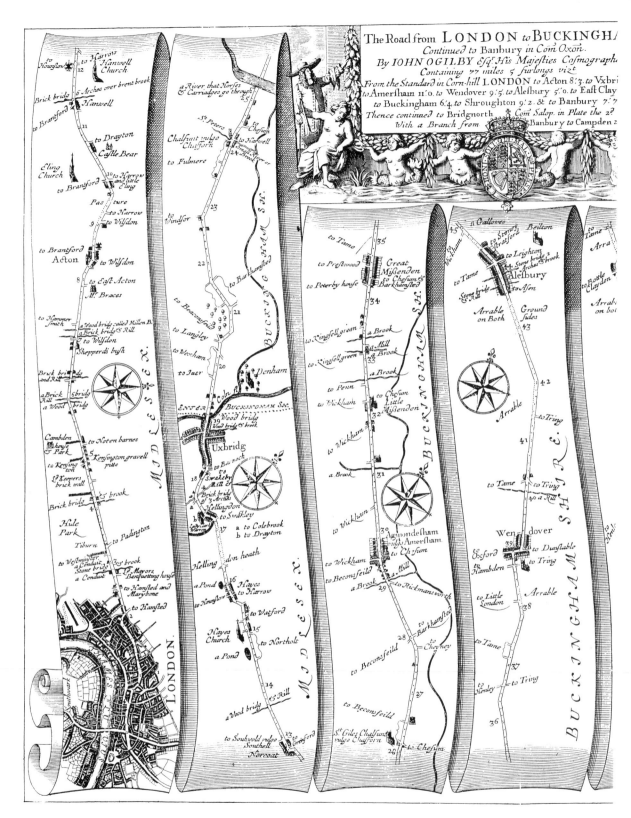

27. *The Buckingham Road* (Uxbridge Road) from a map in Ogilby's *Britannia* (1675).

Transport before the Railway

ON THE UXBRIDGE ROAD

The main thoroughfare linking the two parishes
was the Uxbridge Road, a road with a long history.
It was a major route out of London, first to Uxbridge, then to Oxford and the West Midlands. In
the Middle Ages repair of highways was often prob-
lematic, liability falling usually on the parish or on
the lord of the manor. As a means of regularising
the matter, as far as main roads were concerned,
turnpike trusts were formed, taking over the responsibility for maintenance and having the powers
to levy tolls to pay for it.

The first such turnpike was created on part of the
Great North Road in 1663; the stretch of Uxbridge
Road between Tyburn (Marble Arch) and Uxbridge
was turnpiked in 1715 and much of the rest by 1720.
Toll houses were set up at regular intervals, and one
stood in West Ealing near the Green Man public
house. These individual turnpike trusts remained in
existence until 1826 when all the London trusts
were consolidated by the establishment of the Metropolis Roads Commission Trust, which had an
annual revenue of £60–70,000 and controlled some
172 miles of roads. By 1872 all roads within the metropolitan area were freed from tolls and transferred
to their respective local authorities.

Roads in Ealing, other than those maintained by
the turnpike trusts, were governed by Highway
Trustees established in 1767, but a similar highway
board for Hanwell was not formed until 1885.

28. Lediard's map of the *Great Road from Tybourn to Uxbridge* published in 1750

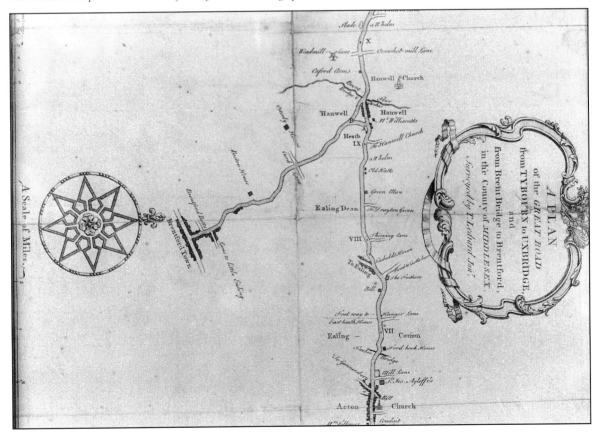

29. *Toll gate in Boston Road, Hanwell* in the 1860s. It stood outside the Royal Victoria Inn and controlled access to the Uxbridge Road turnpike.

THE HEYDAY OF COACHES

Apart from private carriage traffic along the Uxbridge Road there were a number of regular coaches and carriers. The early decades of the nineteenth century have been described as the golden age of the stage coach and there were a great many coach operators and a bewildering number of routes. Coach traffic fell into two categories: the celebrated and romanticised long-distance vehicles with names such as *Retaliator* and *Defiance*, and the more prosaic, but nonetheless useful, short-stages. Long distance coaches and the bustling activity of the post-houses, where horses were changed and travellers sought refreshment, are familiar from the novels of eighteenth and nineteenth century writers. Ealing and Hanwell, of course, were on the route to places west such as Oxford, Birmingham, Banbury, Cheltenham, Gloucester, Worcester and Holyhead, but the long distance traffic only stopped to pick up and set down passengers, not to change horses, because post houses so near to London would have been unwarranted. The *Paul Pry*, for example, which ran daily to Worcester, called at the Bell Inn as did the *Royal Mail*; the *Telegraph*, whose destination was also Worcester, stopped at the Old Hats.

The short stages ran between central London and the suburban fringe and there were a number travelling to and from Uxbridge. The main operator on this route was the Uxbridge firm of Tollits, who in 1819 offered the journey from Holborn in three hours. In that year Ealing was being served by three short-stages a day coming from central London. In 1825 two coaches operated a service between Ealing and the City. During the 1830s the omnibus began to replace the short-stage coach. In 1838–39, at the time the Great Western Railway's London to Bristol line was opened, there were five short-stages operating between Holborn and Uxbridge, four run by various members of the Tollit family, and three omnibuses running between Ealing and the Bank, owned by the Ives family, from the New Inn in St Mary's Road, by the parish church.

The same short-stages served Hanwell as well. Tollit's called at the Duke of York and the King's Arms, and later an omnibus ran between Hanwell and the Bank. The railway was to have a significant impact on the long distance coaches, but its initial effect was much reduced on the convenient short-stages and omnibuses. Still, by 1845, three coaches passed through Ealing and Hanwell to Uxbridge and Wycombe: the 'Prince of Wales' coach to Banbury and Oxford called at the Halfway House in Ealing Dean, and the Ives' omnibuses were making six journeys a day from the Castle and New Inns.

Numerous public houses on the Uxbridge Road served the traffic. The Bell, the Feathers, the Green

30. *The Duke of York* public house, Hanwell Broadway, early in the twentieth century, but not much changed from the coaching days. It has subsequently been rebuilt.

31. *Horse bus* in Ealing Broadway *c*1890.

32. *The Bell Inn*, Uxbridge Road, Ealing.

33. *The Ealing-Hanwell horse bus*.

34. *The Feathers Hotel* in 1860.

Man and the Old Hats, all appear on the 1777 parish map of Ealing. Market gardeners called in the early mornings at the Bell, and the Green Man in West Ealing was a carters' stopping place with stabling, reputably, for a hundred horses.

There were two public houses called the Old Hats, adjacent to each other near the Hanwell parish boundary. The more easterly, later known as the Original Old Hats, was of some antiquity and was described in 1796 as 'a general sauntering place for men and cattle, and the different mixture of farmers, landlords, postillions, stage-coach passengers etc. broiling in the sun', a scene depicted by Cruikshank.

In Hanwell, the Coach and Horses was situated near the bridge over the Brent. In 1838 a 'desperate affray' took place here involving labourers employed in the building of the Great Western Railway. Reflecting the change in transport the inn was renamed The Viaduct.

South of the Uxbridge Road the Bath Road passed through Brentford. The north-south routes, St Mary's Road, Northfield Lane and Gunnersbury Lane, linked Ealing with Brentford, while Boston Lane joined Hanwell and New Brentford. To the north of the Uxbridge Road Hanger Lane went from Ealing Common to Alperton, crossing the Brent near the Fox and Goose, and Castlebar Road from Haven Green to Greenford and Perivale. Green Lane took a northerly route from Ealing Dean to Greenford via Drayton Green and joined the Castlebar Road near the River Brent. Cuckoo Lane joined Hanwell and Greenford.

35. *Travellers at the Old Hats,* from an engraving by Cruikshank. From Woodward's *Eccentric excursions and pictorial sketches* (1796).

36. *The Old Hats or Halfway House*, the more easterly of the two similarly named inns. The entrance to the stable yard can be seen to the right.

37. *Rebuilding Hanwell Bridge* 1906.

LOCAL WATERWAYS

The upkeep of the bridge over the Brent at Hanwell was of major concern. The date of the first bridge here is unknown, although the need to repair it was noted in fourteenth-century records. It was later re-built or repaired in stone but was, however, de-scribed as 'a brick bridge of six arches' on Ogilby's map of 1675. By 1762 the Turnpike Trustees were responsible, and they widened it, and when after 1815 the county took it over, it was widened again. The bridge was faced in stone in 1906.

As for the Brent river itself, it was of little econo-mic value to the locality. It was probably never navigable at any distance from the Thames. Shallow and sluggish in dry months it rapidly filled in wet weather and inundated the meadows of Greenford and Perivale.

The Grand Junction Canal was opened in 1798 to connect the Midlands and London, entering the Thames at Brentford. Later, with the opening of the Paddington arm and the Regent's Canal, a direct line was opened with the London docks. At Brent-ford and Hanwell the course of the river Brent was utilised. The river and canal diverge again near Green Lane in Hanwell, the canal going behind Hanwell Asylum (now Ealing Hospital) towards Southall, passing through the impressive set of locks known as the Hanwell flight, although they are outside the actual parish. Canal-building brought labourers into the area but it appears to have had little long-term economic effect. Hanwell didn't have the brick-earth which was exploited in Northolt and Hayes, although some gravel seems to have been worked in the area west of Boston Road and carried on the canal; the boats were loaded at Hume's wharf, owned by Thomas Hume, who had married the daughter of G.H. Glasse.

An Education Industry

38. *William Dodd* from the painting by John Russell, 1759.

A PLACE OF PRIVATE SCHOOLS

Ealing was an important centre for private schools. Even in 1599 Thomas Haward was running a school here in his father's house, where he tutored eighteen pupils aged from six to seventeen. This style of private tuition continued into the seventeenth and eighteenth centuries, and a number of schoolmasters were licensed to teach in Ealing.

The most notorious of these was undoubtedly the Revd William Dodd, a fashionable London preacher, who taught a few boys at a house near Pope's Cross in the 1760s. One of his pupils was Philip Stanhope, godson and heir of the Earl of Chesterfield, to whom the celebrated letters were written. It was Dodd's forging of Chesterfield's signature on a bond that led to his arrest, trial and execution in 1777. After his death the same building housed a school run by the Revd Samuel Goodenough, whose illustrious pupils included (the later) Viscount Sidmouth and the Earl of Elgin, forever associated with the Parthenon friezes.

A similar establishment was run by the Revd Charles Wallington from a house on Haven Green from 1783 to 1822, and continued by the Revd B. Greenlaw to 1828. Edward Bulwer-Lytton, the novelist, was a pupil. He was to write of Ealing that 'the country around where my good preceptor resided was rural enough for a place so near the metropolis. A walk of somewhat less than a mile, through lanes that were themselves retired and lonely, led to green sequestered meadows, through which the humble Brent crept along its snake-like way'.

GREAT EALING SCHOOL

The largest and longest lived of the early schools was Great Ealing School, which occupied the old rectory beside the parish church. Founded, it is thought, in 1698, its early history is thinly documented until it was taken over in 1791 by the Revd Dr David Nicholas, son-in-law of the rector of Perivale. Thereafter the school achieved considerable fame under him and his sons, George and Francis, and grew in size until there were 200 pupils in 1811 and 365 in 1820. At this period the school was compared favourably with that at Harrow and it seems to have been run on contemporary public school lines. The Revd B.J. Armstrong wrote of it as it had been in the 1830s: 'The school being almost considered a public one, the fagging system was

39. *Great Ealing School*, a view from the playground. The tower of St Mary's church is visible

regularly carried out...the education was first-rate (particularly in the classics) and as the time was judiciously divided, and there was no alternative to learn, the boys progressed rapidly, and the school turned out some bright fellows.' These included Charles Knight, author and publisher, Thomas Huxley, whose father was a mathematics master here, and John Henry Newman, whose brothers were also scholars here. In the early 1800s Louis-Phillipe, later to be the French king, taught mathematics and geography while he was in exile.

By the 1840s the school may have been in decline, but it moved in 1847 to new premises, known as the Owls (from the school crest), on the opposite side of St Mary's Road. In the meantime Thorn House Academy, founded in 1836, occupied what had been the master's house, while Church House school, founded in 1820, was nearby, on the corner of Church Lane and St Mary's Road. These three schools, including Great Ealing, closed around the turn of the century.

The history of Ealing's schools allows us to see many of the characteristics of private schools of this period in a microcosm. As small-scale commercial concerns they were sometimes short-lived, and might pass through the hands of several proprietors with changes of name and style. But they did not operate in a vacuum and, as we shall see, had by necessity to respond to prevailing educational trends.

In 1839 there were at least eleven 'academies', in addition to the 'National' schools run in conjunction with Anglican churches. As late as 1900, long after the 1870 Education Act which established state-funded elementary schools, there were 29 private schools in Ealing.

EDUCATION FOR GIRLS

The nineteenth century saw an increasing number of girls' academies. In 1839 Mary Ann Robinson was running a girls' boarding school in Rochester House, Little Ealing, and by 1866 Mrs Wristbridge had begun the first of her schools, which in 1882 was described as a 'Ladies' Collegiate School' run on the most 'improved principles of the high school system'.

The principal girls' school was Princess Helena

40. *Great Ealing School* in the building known as 'The Owls'. The photograph was taken in the 1860s.

41. Handbill advertising Elthorne Ladies College in West Ealing, 1887.

College, which moved to Ealing from Regent's Park in 1882. Originally founded to educate the orphaned daughters of the clergy and the military, so that they could become governesses, by the time it arrived in Ealing it combined this objective with a high school education for middle class girls. The school was housed in specially constructed premises in Montpelier Road, which were opened by the Princess of Wales. Occupying nine acres, there was accommodation for 55 boarders and 100 day pupils, with a kindergarten for boys and girls. The school stayed in Ealing until 1933, when it moved to Hertfordshire; the buildings were demolished and replaced by Helena Court and Montpelier School.

Harvington School, a girls' school which still remains, illustrates an interesting facet of Victorian education – the German influence. It was originally called Heidelberg College, but changed its name during the First World War. Other schools with German connections were Rolandseck School, whose headmaster was Dr E.F. Marx, whose prospectus claimed that French and German were spoken 'not only during the lessons, but at all times', and Friedenheim School, in Craven Gardens, Uxbridge Road, which also laid stress on languages, although the principals appear to have been English. In 1878 Dr. Aug. Muller PhD of the University of Gottingen proposed to establish a school which would follow 'as far as is practicable, the system pursued at the principal public school in Germany.' He was later to become headmaster of Ealing College.

ELTHORNE LADIES' COLLEGE,

UXBRIDGE ROAD, EALING DEAN, W.,

IN CONNECTION WITH

Eccleston Collegiate School for Boys.

Principal — MRS. SMITH.

The object of this School is to provide a sound, liberal Education for Girls at Moderate Fees.

The Course of Instruction includes the Scriptures, French, German; the various branches of English, including Elementary Drawing.

SPECIAL ATTENTION is paid to Reading, Writing, Spelling, English Grammar, Analysis and Composition, Arithmetic, and Grammatical French and German *throughout* the School.

The System of Education is the same as that adopted in the Modern High Schools, care being taken that every Pupil shall be thoroughly grounded in each subject.

Fees per Term:

Girls over 12 years of age	£2	2 0
Girls under 12 ,, ...	£1	11 6
Stationery ... ... 5s. each extra.		

EXTRA OPTIONAL CHARGES :

Instrumental Music, from	£1	1 0
Shorthand, Book-keeping & Drilling (each) ...	£0	10 6

New Pupils are admitted at any time, and pay from date of entry only.

Full particulars and detailed Prospectuses of both Schools may be obtained on application to the Head Mistress, at the School.

The next Term will commence on Monday, Sept. 5th, 1887, at 10 o'clock.

42. *Princess Helena College*, Montpelier Road, Ealing, from a postcard.

43. The dining room at *Heidelberg College*, later Harvington School, Castlebar Road *c*1905.

NEW TYPES OF SCHOOLS

In the nineteenth century education became more institutionalised and regulated. A series of public examinations were introduced in the 1850s, including that of the College of Preceptors, and the Local Examinations of the Universities of Oxford and Cambridge; there were also entrance examinations for the civil service and military colleges. These tests became standard, and schools were obliged to prepare pupils for them – success in this matter was a yardstick which parents used to evaluate a school. Castle Hill School, for example, claimed in 1893 that 'out of 56 boys entered for the Locals since 1885, 49 have passed, 18 in honours. Out of 14 entered in 1892, 11 passed, three being seniors.'

Careers in the army, navy and civil service were popular. There were a number of military families in Ealing and it is not surprising to see schools and crammers offering coaching towards entrance to military and naval colleges. In 1872 Dr Northcott had a military college at Rochester House where pupils were prepared mainly for Sandhurst, Woolwich and the Royal Naval College. Harrow View School in Cleveland Road, begun in the 1890s, had a naval emphasis and prepared boys for public schools and the Naval College at Osborne.

As classics gave ground to scientific and commer-cial subjects, so the curriculum changed during the nineteenth century. In 1896 Castlebar Court School, in Queen's Walk, claimed it had 'first class laboratories for practical work in chemistry and electricity', and Professor Hoffert offered in 1896 an engineering education covering chemistry, metallurgy, electricity, physics, geology, mining, surveying and drawing to boys over fifteen and special preparation for entrance to the Royal Colleges of Science and Mines. Beside the commercial subjects increasingly offered by many schools, there were a number of specifically commercial colleges. Ealing Commercial College was opened in 1888 as a day and boarding school in West Ealing on the corner of Uxbridge and Eccleston roads. In 1912 Ealing Secretarial College taught girls commercial French and German, shorthand, typewriting and bookkeeping. Branches of Clark's College and Pitman's College were operating in Ealing before the First World War.

Preparatory schools, to prepare boys for entrance to public schools, were also in Ealing. Durston House, in Castlebar Road, founded in 1886, and Hamilton House in Florence Road, founded in 1905, still survive.

The first Catholic school in Ealing was SS Joseph & Peter in Mattock Lane, run by Father O'Halloran

44. Boys in the playground at *Ealing Grammar School*, the successor to Byron House School, *c*1900. This private school, in The Park, is not to be confused with the Ealing County Grammar School.

BYRON HOUSE SCHOOL,

✢ THE PARK, ✢

EALING. W.

A Classical and Modern Commercial School.

Session ending *Dec^t 20th* 18*92*.

This Prize was awarded to

M. E. R. Jones

For being *1st* in *3rd* Class

of *French.*

Principal: B. BRUCESMITH, F.S. Sc., &c.

PALMAM QUI MERUIT FERAT.

J. NEWNS, PRINTER, ETC., GROVE BAZAAR, EALING.

45. *Byron House School* – a bookplate from a prize book, 1892.

in the 1890s. St Anne's Convent School occupied Ealing Park from 1903, and the Convent of the Augustinians Ladies' School opened in The Elms, Hillcrest Road, in 1915. From 1923 Lourdes Mount was the fifth school to use Rochester House. A boys' school, now known as St Benedict's, was opened by the Benedictines in 1902.

An unusual educational initiative was the establishment in 1864 of the Ealing Deanery Middle Class school, promoted by the Ealing Ruri-Decanal Association with the aim of providing a school in which religious education would be a significant part of the curriculum, but which would avoid the worst aspects of the privately owned schools. This plan caused dissension within the Association as well as, unsurprisingly, incurring the antagonism of the masters of the existing private high schools. Taking boarders and day pupils, it was located in the High Street, New Brentford, but it never attracted sufficient pupils to make it viable, and it closed in 1879.

The number of schools offering boarding facilities indicates that pupils came from some distance. Indeed, many came from families in Britain's far-flung empire. Ealing's connections with India were strong, and a number of ex-Indian army officers and civil servants retired here. In 1861, during the Easter vacation, of the ten pupils remaining at Great Ealing

46. *Ealing College* moved from St Mary's Road to a new building on the corner of Hamilton Road and Uxbridge Road in 1880. It was later known as Hermosa School and then the Proprietary School. An iron church provides additional accommodation.

47. *Durston House Preparatory School* pupils and staff, *c*1890.

School over the holiday, five had been born in India and two in America. Mrs R.B. Stranack, of Netley Villas, received 'a limited number of young gentlemen, children of parents residing in India or elsewhere from the age of four to twelve, to board and educate' (1875). Whinrey House School in Eaton Rise was a 'desirable home for Indian and orphan children' (1888). Heidelberg College advertised in 1912 that it made special arrangements for Anglo-Indian and colonial children, and Llanberis School in Mount Avenue described itself in 1896 as an Anglo-Indian school, and was 'principally open to the daughters of officers as boarders or day pupils, but admission is also permitted to daughters of civilians at home and abroad'.

SOME HANWELL SCHOOLS

Hanwell did not have Ealing's concentration of schools, but during the later nineteenth century always had about three private schools at any one time, of which one was for girls. The Revd John Bond ran a school at Brent Lodge in the 1820s, but the best known school was Hanwell College, begun in 1832 and closed in the 1880s. This was conducted by the Revd J.A. Emerton, the curate of St Mary's, Hanwell and occupied substantial premises where Manor Court now joins Church Road; in the 1870s it offered preparation for the public schools, professional examinations and for the 'higher branches of commerce'. Brent Hill Collegiate School in Lower Boston Road had separate departments for boys and girls.

48. A fête champêtre at Hanwell College in the 1840s.

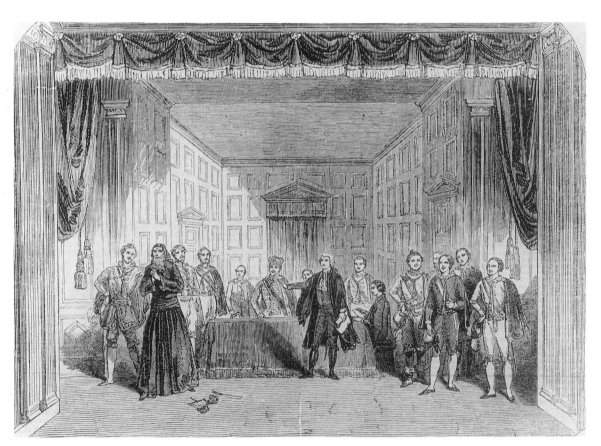

49. A production of *The Merchant of Venice* at Hanwell Collegiate School in December 1848. A notice appeared in *The Lady's Newspaper*.

The Profession of Madness

HANWELL ASYLUM

The Middlesex County Asylum, generally known as Hanwell Asylum, was built in 1831, not in Hanwell as such, but in the precinct of Norwood, now Southall. However, because the hospital stood much nearer to Hanwell than any other centre of population, it has always been linked to Hanwell.

The Asylum forms part of a movement to provide better and more regulated facilities for the mentally ill. Under the terms of the County Asylums Act of 1808 magistrates could authorise the building of asylums by a county, or a group of counties, at the expense of the county ratepayers, to accommodate pauper lunatics maintained by their native parishes. Land, some 55 acres, was bought from the Earl of Jersey, a major local landowner whose estates included Osterley Park. The Asylum was originally planned to accommodate 450 patients, but escalating costs forced a reduction to 300. The architect of the building was William Anderson and the builder William Cubitt.

At first the buildings consisted of long low brick blocks arranged on three sides of a square with octagonal towers on the two open ends and in the middle of the third side. The wards were on the ground and upper floors, but as early as 1839, when the Asylum was already overcrowded (the number of patients had risen to 791), the basements were also used for patients. 'Airing courts' – enclosed areas for obligatory outdoor exercise – were situated behind the main blocks. A massive and somewhat forbidding gatehouse fronted the Uxbridge Road.

Hanwell Asylum was really a self-contained town. Patients worked under the supervision of

50. *View of the Hanwell Asylum* as originally built.

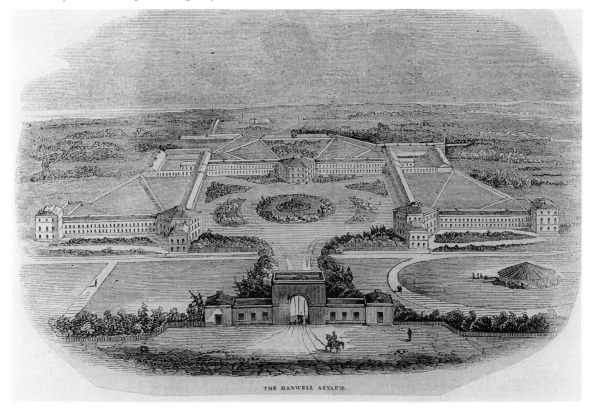

THE HANWELL ASYLUM.

experienced tradesmen; horses, cows, pigs and poultry were kept and fruit and vegetables grown; the buildings were lit by gas produced on site from coal brought by boat on the Grand Junction Canal to the Asylum's own dock; facilities included a brewery, dairy, laundry, kitchens, and workshops for basketmaking, upholstery, furniture repair, carpentry, dressmaking, tailoring and shoemaking. At first water was drawn direct from the canal but in 1832 and 1834 cholera caused the deaths of fifteen patients; thereafter water was filtered, but in 1842 a well was sunk to a depth of 213 feet at a cost of £1,500.

The first superintendent was Dr (later Sir) William Ellis. He believed in the humane treatment of the patients and that those who were able should be engaged in useful work. But in 1838, following a disagreement with the management committee, he resigned. His replacement was Dr John Conolly, an innovator in the treatment of the mentally ill. He pursued a system of non-restraint and he encouraged games and outdoor recreations, including supervised outings. Aside from the superintendent, there were in 1840 fifteen other staff and 75 servants, including 19 male keepers (attendants) and 29 female servants. The 1851 Census for Hanwell district (which did not include the actual Asylum) includes 19 individuals employed at the Asylum, five of whom were attendants not at home on the night of the Census, presumably on night duty.

52. Gateway to the Hanwell Asylum. The spire of the chapel is visible in the background.

51. The Fire Brigade at Hanwell Asylum.

53. Patients at Hanwell Asylum celebrate Twelfth Night, 1848. Such events were part of the policy of non-restraint.

54. John Conolly.

One of the most interesting developments at the Asylum was the Bazaar. It was discovered that many of the female patients were skilled in fine needlework, and it was decided to purchase materials which could be made up by these patients and sold either in a bazaar or made to order. The profits from this economic and therapeutic activity were spent on comforts for the patients.

The Asylum continued to grow and although there were plans to erect a second building on an adjacent site, the second Middlesex Asylum was eventually built instead in Colney Hatch, Hornsey, in 1851. At Hanwell additional wings were added in 1838, a new chapel with clock tower and spire built in 1880, and over the years additional accommodation was provided so that, by 1916, the number of inmates had risen to 2750.

Changes in mental health care has resulted in the reduction of patients at the Asylum, or St Bernard's Hospital as it is now called. Some of its buildings have been demolished and Ealing Hospital now occupies part of the site.

THE LATE DR. CONOLLY, RESIDENT PHYSICIAN OF HANWELL LUNATIC ASYLUM.

55. *Elm Grove House* in 1870, when it became the Royal India Asylum.

PRIVATE ASYLUMS

Hanwell Asylum admitted the poor, but private asylums catered for those families which had means. After Conolly gave up his post at the Asylum in 1844 he ran a private asylum at Lawn House, Hanwell, until 1866. The 1851 Census shows four patients 'of unsound mind' here; two other such asylums appear in Hanwell the same year, the largest of which had eight patients.

Ealing's own asylum was more specialised. In 1870 the India Office purchased Elm Grove House from Mrs Spencer Perceval, the daughter-in-law of the former Prime Minister, Spencer Perceval. The East India Company had provided an asylum for its employees at Pembroke House, Hackney, but when it was purchased by the Great Eastern Railway, the India Office, which had taken over the Company's powers after the Indian Mutiny of 1859, looked around for a new home.

Elm Grove was converted at a cost of £11,700 under the direction of Sir Matthew Digby Wyatt and it opened in August 1870 as the Royal India Asylum. Its superintendent was Dr Thomas B. Christie, formerly the assistant at Pembroke House. He became an important local figure, especially active in the Conservative Party and the Primrose League. Entry to the Asylum was restricted after 1872 to military personnel. In 1892 the house and estate was sold to Leopold de Rothschild and the remaining 75 inmates transferred elsewhere; two years later the house was demolished and the land developed.

The Arrival of the Railway

The building of the Great Western Railway main line from London to Bristol in the late 1830s was a significant event for both parishes. Such a route had been proposed as early as 1825 but nothing came of it. Interest was renewed following the success of the Liverpool & Manchester Railway, which opened in 1830, and planning in earnest began in 1833 when a Bristol committee appointed Isambard Kingdom Brunel as engineer, and the name Great Western Railway was adopted. However, it was not until 1835 that the Act of Parliament authorising the line was obtained.

There was some local opposition – it saw no advantage and resented the disruption caused by the works and the invasion of navvies. Nevertheless, the Ealing vestry, some of whose members no doubt stood to gain from the purchase of their lands, voted in favour by eleven votes to four.

Construction actually started at Hanwell with the building of a viaduct over the Brent river, one of the major engineering projects on the line. This was named the Wharncliffe Viaduct, in honour of Lord Wharncliffe, the chairman of the company; it was 860ft long, 65ft high and built of brick with stone piers, by the famous railway contractor Grissell & Peto; it was completed in 1837.

Much of the Ealing section runs in a shallow cutting, its course presumably determined by the nature of the soil, which is light and gravelly, whereas it would be clay further north. This alignment, running through farmland just north of the Uxbridge Road, did not necessitate the demolition of any property. Landowners were compensated and the vestry received £150 for the loss of common rights at Haven Green.

Stations were built at Hanwell and Ealing. On 9 January 1838 G.H. Cribbs, a GWR engineer, reported that 'Ealing station is in a very unfinished state; Hanwell embankment is not yet completed on either side'. And although the railway commenced operations on 4 June 1838, the stations were not open until December that year.

The station at Ealing was modest, but attractive, its appearance, at least in illustrations, enhanced by the farmland that still surrounded it. Ealing Station was in the cutting, but the one at Hanwell, again an unpretentious building, was on an embankment, close to the eastern end of the Wharncliffe Viaduct. Both stations were replaced in the 1870s and much of the later Hanwell buildings survive.

Geographically the area was greatly affected by the railway. Ealing was divided along an east-west axis, and seven bridges were required to accommodate existing roads and paths. These were, from east to west, Hanger Lane, Ealing Broadway (Haven Green), Spring Bridge, Longfield Avenue, St Leonard's Road, Drayton Bridge, and later the West Ealing footbridge, familiarly known as Jacob's Ladder.

The building of the line parallel and close to the Uxbridge Road isolated a strip of land which became less suited to agriculture, but attractive for development, but while the new railway stimulated some building it did not immediately create a commuter suburb at either Ealing or Hanwell. Indeed the mechanism linking railway building and suburban development is not nearly as simple as has sometimes been made out. In the case of the GWR, in the decades following 1838 there were not enough commuters, even had the railway provided a full service, which it didn't until the 1870s.

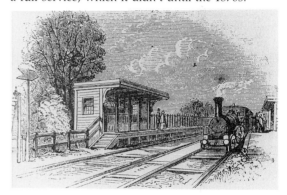

56. The first Hanwell Station.

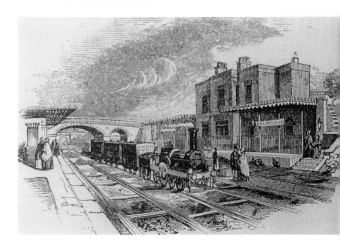

57. The first Ealing Station.

58. *Wharncliffe Viaduct.*

59. *Ealing Haven Station, c*1840. Artist unknown.

60. Houses built on the glebe land, Castlebar Road, 1860s. A postcard *c*1900.

A New Suburb

The arrival of the railway did not immediately transform Ealing and Hanwell, but some building did take place in the decade following 1840. This marks the beginning of suburban development.

In 1841 Ealing had 608 inhabited and 49 uninhabited houses, whilst only nine were under construction. A decade later there were 711 in existence with 16 building, an increase overall of 54. Growth then was modest and though probably noticeable to residents not intrusive since it was spread over a number of sites, not necessarily near the railway station.

An obvious site for building was the Ashton House estate, situated between Uxbridge Road and Ealing Green, where Bond Street was later built. John Ibbotson owned the house and grounds which had frontages both on Uxbridge Road and Mattock Lane. In 1846 he made an agreement with a local builder, Thomas Nye, which subdivided the western part of the property into building plots of an average width of 32ft, to be let on 99-year leases. By 1851 Ibbotson had moved out of Ashton House which was in use then as a school. Development of the Uxbridge Road frontage was complete by the

mid–1860s, but only half the Mattock Lane plots had been taken up. On the west side of the High Street building took place at the northern end, on the corner with the Uxbridge Road and this included the Railway Hotel.

The most individual, but small-scale, project of the 1840s was in the Park, on an 11-acre field owned by Sir Edward Kerrison. The Park is on the east side of St Mary's Road, some distance from the station. Five pairs of semi-detached villas were built to the designs of Sydney Smirke, architect of the circular Reading Room at the British Museum. This symmetrical group of elegant Italianate villas is unlike other building in Ealing and contrasts with the rest of the road which is later and much less distinctive.

More schemes began in the 1850s. A small area of the glebe land (five acres) on Castlebar Hill, a few minutes walk from Ealing Station, was sold by the Ecclesiastical Commissioners for £1,220 in 1852 to S.L. Matthews. He completed two houses in 1853 but the remainder of the land was sold on to other developers, one of whom was William Harris, a Kensington publican, who also acquired land in Hanwell and West Ealing. Nineteen houses on the east side of Castlebar Road had been built by the mid–1860s.

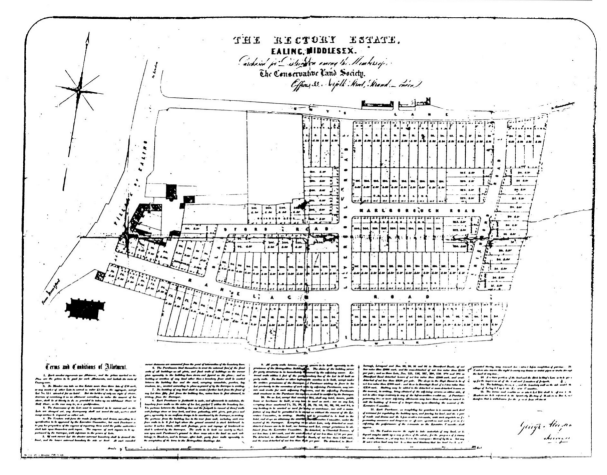

61. *Rectory Estate, Ealing.* Plan of estate drawn by W.J. Green in 1868.

The removal of Great Ealing School from its position near the church to new premises on the opposite side of St Mary's Road in 1847, freed new land for building. The Rectory estate was bought in the 1850s by the Conservative Freehold Land Society which, in 1853, tried unsuccessfully to obtain season ticket concessions for its clients from the Great Western Railway. Progress on the estate was slow and by the mid–1860s only a few houses were complete, although Ranelagh, Blandford, Liverpool, Marlborough and Richmond Roads had been laid out. The development of this estate, some distance from the Uxbridge Road and the station, was bound to be slow. This is confirmed by a notice which appeared in *Acworth's Monthly Advertiser* in 1862, advertising that 'several valuable plots of freehold land on the above estate are now offered for sale, or on lease at a small ground rent, thus giving a rare opportunity to build. As the demand for house

property is rapidly increasing in this improving village, persons wishing to become owners of property will do well to embrace the present opportunity. Money advances may also be obtained at reasonable terms.' There were still gaps in some of the roads as late as the 1890s.

On the strip of land between Uxbridge Road and the railway the Wood family estate built five pairs of villas, known as Craven Villas; these had a rear access road, presumably for stabling.

A sign of the changing character of Ealing was the decision of Ealing Vestry in 1851 to provide street lighting for that part of the parish between the Boys' National School, just south of the church, and the Feathers Hotel.

By 1861 the number of houses in Ealing had risen to 1007 and in Hanwell, where new development was concentrated on the Uxbridge Road and Boston Road, the increase since 1841 was from 263 to 335.

Burying the Dead

In Victorian England burying the dead became a significant problem. A dramatic increase in population and the growth of urban areas put existing burial grounds attached to churches, particularly those in central London, under pressure. The insanitary state of some of these overcrowded urban churchyards was a danger to health, especially during epidemics. In addition to these practical problems there was the religious dimension: non-conformists were anxious to have burial grounds not tied to the established church.

The situation prompted a number of innovations. One was the establishment of private cemeteries, run on commercial lines: the first of these in London was at Kensal Green, opened in 1830. Another was the purchase by central London parishes of land out of town to provide burial space. Two such extra-mural cemeteries were located in Hanwell: on the north side of the Uxbridge Road, close to the Ealing boundary, was a burial ground for the parish of St Mary Abbot, Kensington, opened in 1855; opposite was that of St George, Hanover Square, opened in 1854. In both cases the cemeteries follow the pattern that developed during the nineteenth century: they were landscaped as parks, and the architecture is almost always Gothic, as, usually, were churches built from the 1840s. Buildings included two chapels in each cemetery, one for the Church of England, the other for non-conformists, and gatekeepers' lodges. These examples of Victorian architecture are well preserved – they are now the responsibility of the London boroughs of Kensington and Westminster.

But Hanwell, too, needed more burial space and a Burial Board was formed in 1881. Rather than open its own cemetery the Board made an arrangement to use the two extra-mural cemeteries described above, but eventually this ceased to be practical and the Urban District Council, which had taken over the Board's functions, arranged to use Greenford Park Cemetery instead – this was originally a private cemetery, that had later been taken over by Greenford Council.

Ealing had the same problem. A Burial Board was established for Ealing and Old Brentford in 1858 and a site for a cemetery purchased in 1860. This was off South Ealing Road and was deliberately chosen to be between the two areas. The eight-acre ground was laid out in 1861, furnished again with Gothic chapels for Anglicans and non-conformists. It continues in use as the South Ealing cemetery.

62. *Westminster Cemetery lodge*, Hanwell.

63. The chapels at *Ealing Cemetery*.

64. *Ealing and Old Brentford cemetery* in South Ealing *c*1900. The photograph seems to have been taken from the roof of the adjacent refuse destructor.

The Central London District School

The building of the Central London District School in Hanwell in 1857 was a major event, not unlike the building of the Hanwell Asylum some twenty-five years earlier. And although both establishments brought about an increase in local population and employment they were essentially closed, self-supporting communities.

The School was one of several such designed to educate those whose families had ended up in workhouses. The Poor Law Unions (groups of parishes) set up by the Poor Law Amendment Act of 1834, were given powers to combine with other Unions to provide schools for the children in their care.

The Central London District School was funded by the City of London, the East London and the St Saviour's Unions. Originally an existing school in Norwood was purchased for the purpose but this rapidly became overcrowded. When cholera struck in 1853, 24 children were taken ill and 14 died. The Poor Law Board, the Government department which supervised the work of the Unions, encour-

aged the District to find a new site of fifty to sixty acres with good communications, and in June 1855 the District offered £12,000 for the eastern part of Hanwell Park Estate, which the owner, Mr Millard, accepted. An architectural competition was held in which Messrs Tress and Chambers were successful. The cost of the buildings was estimated at £35,000 and the foundation stone was laid in September 1856.

The school was not enthusiastically received by many local residents. Complaints were made about damage to roads during building operations, and there were fears that the sewage from the school would badly pollute the River Brent.

In October 1857 the staff and pupils moved in and Mr Aubin, who had been in charge of the school at Norwood, was its first superintendent. There were 67 staff in 1861, comprising teachers, craft instructors and domestics. The children's time was divided between formal school lessons and the 'working division' where they were taught useful trades. As these were children of the poorest families the tendency was to provide education and training suitable for their position in life: boys were mainly taught agriculture and manual trades, and girls domestic work. Later in the century, with changing educational attitudes, the curriculum became more academic. There was also military style drill for both sexes, and the boys were taught musical instruments and organised into bands which had engagements at local social functions; they also provided a recruiting ground for Army musicians. Some child-

65. *The Central London District School*, Hanwell. The tree-lined avenue that led up to the main entrance is on the left of the picture; the clock tower was, and still is, visible for some distance.

66. (Overleaf) A mealtime at the Central London District School *c*1900.

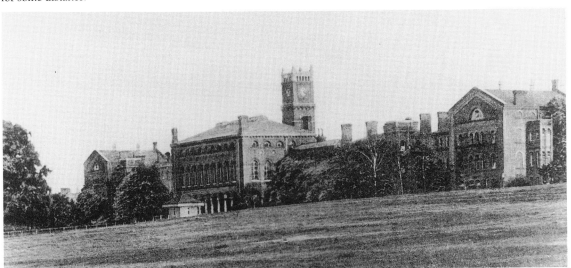

67. The main building of the Central School. The clock tower was added in 1880.

68. The infirmary of the Central School. In a boarding school this size a separate infirmary was a necessity. In the 1870s ophthalmia had been endemic and separate isolation huts had to be built.

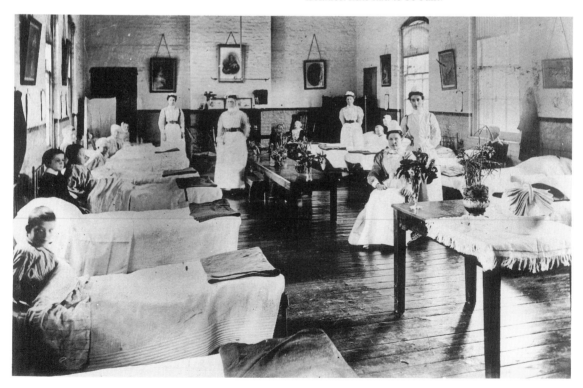

ren were at the school a long time, while others came for a number of short stays, depending on family circumstances. As a result the school population fluctuated, but there were often over 1000 pupils, the best-known being Charlie Chaplin.

The central buildings, reached by a long tree-lined avenue, formed an imposing group on the crest of the hill overlooking the Brent valley. The main three-storey block was in an Italianate style with a pillared entrance. A number of extensions were built during the nineteenth century and by 1900 the then 140-acre site contained classrooms, residential blocks, an infirmary, and a sewage and a gas works. The remaining land was farmed by the tenant of Cuckoo Farm and provided fresh produce for the school. Water came from a well, pumped to a tower by steam power.

The poor law unions were finally abolished in 1929 and the school was transferred the next year to the London County Council. The LCC decided to rationalise its many schools and homes and in 1932 the closure of Cuckoo school, as it was generally known, was announced. It was closed in 1933, mostly demolished, and its grounds used for a housing estate; the main block survives and is now a community centre.

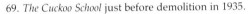

69. *The Cuckoo School* just before demolition in 1935.

Slow Development

AUSTIN'S DREAM

The 1860s saw a housing boom in London. In Ealing the number of houses, according to the censuses, increased from 1007 to 1885, with major development on the Oxford and Windsor Roads on the south side of Uxbridge Road, at Eaton Rise to the north-west of Haven Green and further building on the Rectory estate. Eaton Rise was built from about 1868 by John Galloway of Kilburn, who bought a single long, thin field (shaped like a spearhead) and laid out houses on both sides of the road and on the adjacent part of Castlebar Road. Most of his houses were leasehold, and at rateable values, modest by Ealing standards, varying from £47 to £6 0, while those in Oxford and Windsor Roads were at £47 or below.. In Hanwell the pace was slower and only 183 houses were built: sizeable development here did not take place until the 1870s and 1880s.

The principal speculative development of the 1860s was that undertaken in north Ealing by Henry de Bruno Austin, a co-opted member of the Ealing Board of Health from 1864–67. By 1867, however, he was already threatened with financial ruin and his estate was being administered under the Bankruptcy Act. Austin had debts of £40,000, and he was

70. Panorama of Austin's proposed estate at Castle Hill, early 1860s. Kent Gardens is on the right, the train in the background is on the North Metropolitan line, which was never built.

EALING, MIDDLESEX.

THE REMAINING PORTION OF A VALUABLE

FREEHOLD ESTATE,

ADMIRABLY ADAPTED FOR

VILLAS OF A MODERATE CLASS.

Particulars and Conditions of Sale
OF

TWENTY

BUILDING PLOTS,

LYING BETWEEN

EALING GREEN AND EALING COMMON,

SEVERAL OF THE LOTS ABUTTING THEREON, THE OTHERS HAVING

FRONTAGES TO GROVE ROAD,

AND A NEW ROAD THROUGH THE ESTATE,

WHICH HAS BEEN LATELY FORMED. THE PLOTS VARYING FROM

A QUARTER OF AN ACRE TO ONE ACRE EACH,

Many of them adorned with fine Chestnut, Beech, and other highly ornamental Forest Trees, and rare Shrubs, which have been carefully kept for many Years, and the value of the Plots greatly enhanced thereby.

The Sub-soil is chiefly gravel, and the situation dry, healthy, and most desirable, being in the most elevated and best part of the Village of Ealing.

Within Five Minutes' Walk of the Railway Station, on the Great Western Railway, 5¾ Miles from Paddington, and by lines now in the course of formation will be in direct communication with the City, Pimlico, and all parts of London and the Country.

Affording a favourable opportunity to those wishing to build for Occupation or Investment, and well adapted for the creation of Ground Rents.

WHICH WILL BE SOLD BY AUCTION, BY

MESSRS.

CHINNOCK & GALSWORTHY,

AT THE MART, OPPOSITE THE BANK OF ENGLAND,

On TUESDAY, JUNE 10th, 1862,

AT TWELVE O'CLOCK, IN TWENTY LOTS.

71. Sale Catalogue of building plots in Grange Road and Grove Road 1862, between Ealing Green and Ealing Common.

finally adjudged bankrupt in 1872. His scheme thus ended in disaster, but not before it had made a distinctive mark on local geography.

His plan was an ambitious one. Between 1862 and 1864 Austin leased 190 acres from two owners, C.P. Millard, who owned Brent, Drayton and Pitshanger Farms, and F.C. Swinden, the owner of Castlebar Park. This large parcel of land stretched from Scotch Common in the north to the railway line, at the place where West Ealing station would later be built.

By 1866 Austin had begun a pattern of 50ft wide roads, with gas and water mains, but without mains drainage. The west side of Kent Gardens was laid out with fourteen semi-detached houses, while Cleveland Gardens (now part of Argyle Road) had three pairs of houses and one villa, and Cleveland Road a few detached villas. The rentals for these houses, which each had eight to ten bedrooms, were between £150 and £250 per annum, and rateable values were as high as £144.

The success of this estate of superior middle-class housing rested on the attraction of suitable tenants. Austin probably anticipated that the GWR would open a new station at West Ealing (which it did, but not until 1871), or that the plan before Parliament in 1866 for a North Metropolitan line would include a station near to the north of the estate. The panoramic view that Austin prepared shows roads laid out with substantial villas and an area of private gardens, like those in London squares. In the far distance, a train approaches a station on what was presumably the proposed North Metropolitan line.

In the event this line was never built and early residents of the estate had to depend on the existing GWR station at Haven Green. The houses had such high rentals that few could be tempted to take them, when they could probably afford instead more fashionable areas closer to London. The inhabitants of Kent Gardens in 1871 included Austin himself; Alexander Forbes, assistant secretary of the Great Northern and other railway companies; a civil servant; a retired merchant; and two people of independent means. Alexander Hemsley, clerk to the Local Board and a solicitor with a substantial practice, lived in adjoining Cleveland Road. Many of these may well have kept their own carriages. Unfortunately, at this time, these houses could not be connected to the main sewage system, which only extended south of the railway line, and the cess pits, on which the residents had to rely were a source of complaint for some years.

With Austin's bankruptcy parts of the estate were sold in 1869 to land companies, but there was a

72. *Nos. 4–5 Kent Gardens*, shortly before demolition in 1963.

considerable delay before the street plan he had laid out acquired all its houses. Those built in the 1880s and 1890s were more modest than Austin had envisaged, but the church, shown on his panorama as the focal point of the estate, was built (St Stephen, 1876).

THE CASTLE HILL ESTATE

The adjacent land on Castle Hill belonged to the Kent House estate. This was originally the site of Castlehill Lodge, at one time owned by the Duke of Kent. The estate, whose history is well-documented, was owned by the Wetherall family after the Duke died encumbered with debt. During the 1860s Austin was tenant of the house.

A consortium acquired the estate in 1870. This group comprised Alfred Prest, E.J. Pearce, a schoolmaster, and Charles Jones, surveyor to the Local Board. It paid £3,000 for part of the land, but Wetherall appears to have advanced the price on mortgage to them. At the same time Thomas Elliot Harrison bought the house itself, together with the immediate grounds, for £5,500 and in 1871 he purchased a further piece of land for £6,000.

Development of this estate was slow. Victoria Road was laid out across the site and plots changed hand before even the first house was built and sold. In 1880 Harrison sold his house, grounds and land to the north of the house, to the British Land Company for £13,500 and the next year the company was offering 156 plots at a price equivalent to £1,200 per acre, fronting Castlebar Park, Victoria Road and Pitshanger Lane. But even this development was slow and by the 1890s only a few houses were completed. The last infilling did not take place until the 1930s.

Castlehill Lodge, an 1840s building, survived and is the basis of the St David's Home for Disabled Servicemen, which opened in 1918.

73. Plan of building plots on the Castle Hill (Kent House) estate, 1870s. The plots are coloured to show the holdings of the three joint owners.

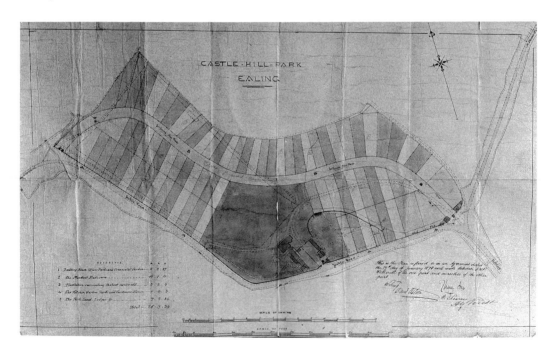

74. *Haven Green* c1880. The second GWR station is on the right, the first MDR station to the left.

More Railways

EXPANDING THE GREAT WESTERN

The GWR had come to Ealing and Hanwell in the late 1830s but in the next thirty years the pace of suburbanisation had been slow. Part of the reason for this may be attributed to the GWR timetable, and the building of the terminus at Paddington on the western fringe of London, neither of which encouraged commuting from further afield.

The inadequacy of the GWR service to the Ealing area prompted a number of other railway projects, such as the proposed North Metropolitan line. More significantly for Ealing 1863 saw the opening of the Metropolitan Line, the first underground railway in the world, from Farringdon to Paddington. The Metropolitan was closely associated with the GWR, at least initially, and their lines gave passengers to Paddington access to the City by a limited number of through trains. After early difficult relations between the two companies an Act of Parliament in 1869 enabled the GWR to run twelve through trains in each direction.

1863 also saw the GWR inaugurate a service to Victoria via the newly-built West London Extension Railway. Trains began at Southall and the journey time was only forty minutes from Ealing, despite the circuitous route which twice crossed the Thames. There were, however, only eight trains

each day in each direction, and the earliest from Ealing did not arrive at Victoria until 9.25am. But these two improvements generated an increase of up to 164% in passenger journeys between Ealing and London. The GWR opened a new station (originally called Castle Hill) at West Ealing in 1871 and this, unlike that at Haven Green which was exclusively for passengers, had a goods depot and coal sidings.

But still the frequency of trains was only two per hour and in the face of much criticism the GWR had to reconsider its attitude to suburban traffic. They promised a better service once the doubling of the tracks had been completed: this would enable express trains to use one track and suburban trains to use the other. This work was a major undertaking since it involved the construction of new platforms, the widening of cuttings, bridges and viaducts, including the Wharncliffe Viaduct at Hanwell. The original intention was to carry this work only to Acton but it went eventually as far as Slough. Unlike the original main line the new 'slow' tracks were laid to standard gauge, and not to the GWR's idiosyncratic broad gauge. At the same time new stations were provided at Ealing and Hanwell.

This new suburban service was launched in 1878 and it provided ten extra trains per day in each direction, which meant that a total of 32 trains per day went to Paddington of which 13 ran through to Moorgate.

75. Passengers awaiting the arrival of a Paddington-bound train at West Ealing in 1916.

76. A local train stands at the westbound slow platform, West Ealing, in 1916. The fast lines are on the left.

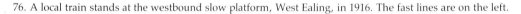

RIVAL LINES

At the same time other railway lines were being mooted. In 1877 three Bills were introduced into Parliament. The first was the Harrow and West End, which proposed a branch from the GWR at Ealing to Roxeth and Harrow. This was rejected as were similar Bills in later years. The second was the Ealing and Kew Bridge railway, which was to run from the LSWR and North London at Kew, past Clayponds, to cross the Ealing Road near Pope's Cross and pass through the market gardens to a terminus in Northfield Lane near St John's church. This proposal also failed to win approval.

The third Bill was that for an Ealing extension to the Metropolitan District Railway. The MDR had been authorised in 1864 to complete what is now the Underground Inner Circle route with a line from South Kensington to Tower Hill. By 1868 the line was open between South Kensington and Westminster but in 1871 the MDR and the Metropolitan parted company and the District pursued its policy of encouraging suburban traffic. The MDR's eastern terminus became Mansion House, its line from Westminster running under the newly-built Victoria Embankment. Its extension to Hammersmith was opened in 1874 and, using the LSWR line, to Richmond in 1877. But the MDR was anxious to open further branches to feed its main route to the West End and the City. Ealing, a growing neighbourhood, was a natural target for this policy, especially as only three miles of new track would be required to link Ealing with the existing line at Turnham Green.

This three miles of track was the substance of the Ealing Extension Bill. A terminus was to be built on Haven Green to the north of the GWR station, and intermediate stations opened at Acton Green (now Chiswick Park), Mill Hill Park (now Acton Town) and at Ealing Common & West Acton (now Ealing Common).

The main opposition to the Bill came, unsurprisingly, from the GWR and other railway companies, but the only local landowner to object was Baron Rothschild, across whose Gunnersbury estate the line would pass. But public opinion in Ealing seems to have been favourable, as was the local press:

'The boon that such a line would be to our town is obvious. It would give a service of trains, certainly at regular, probably at frequent intervals,

77. *North Ealing Station*, standing amidst the fields in 1902.

78. *Northfields Station c*1912. The Ealing District laundry is behind the left-hand platform.

and all these trains would run through to the heart of the city by a route in great part open air and with day light stations. It would also enable us to travel direct to suburbs that can only be reached at present by a roundabout way with a change of carriage en route: we mean the important neighbourhoods of Hammersmith, South Kensington and Brompton.' (*Middlesex County Times*, 9 February 1876)

At the public meeting held at Christchurch school prior to the Parliamentary consideration much dissatisfaction with the GWR was expressed, though this was before the introduction of the company's new suburban timetable. Residents were keen to see competition in the hope that the GWR would improve. Certainly the direct route to the West End that the MDR offered was attractive, and a show of hands at the meeting indicated that as many people wanted to go to the West End as to the City.

The Ealing extension was opened on 1 July 1879. It was said at the time, with a certain amount of journalistic overstatement, to be the most important event in Ealing since the building of the GWR forty years before. The journey to Mansion House was advertised as 43 minutes – no faster than the GWR service due to the extra intermediate stations.

This was not the end of railway developments in Ealing, nor of the MDR's ambitions. The Hounslow and Metropolitan Railway Act of 1880 authorised the building of a 5½-mile branch from the Ealing extension near Ealing Common to the Bath Road

opposite Hounslow barracks. The MDR was to work, manage and maintain the line, which crossed south Ealing. Stations were built at Boston Road, Osterley and South Ealing, which opened up the southern parts of Ealing and Hanwell for full development. After the line was electrified in 1907 a halt was opened at Northfield Lane, rebuilt as a full station in 1911. The last MDR line – to Harrow and Uxbridge – joined the existing tracks near Ealing Common, and a station was opened, amidst the fields, in 1903 (see illustration).

To the north the GWR built a branch to link the main line through Ealing with a new line through Greenford. Much of its route is along the parish boundary between Ealing and Hanwell and stations at Castlebar Park and Drayton Green encouraged development on both sides.

Horsedrawn transport carried passengers to and from the stations. A cab rank stood on Haven Green, and buses ran between the Railway Hotel, Ealing and Acton station, between Ealing MDR station and the Duke of York, Hanwell, and between Ealing and Kew Bridge.

79. GWR train at Trumpers Crossing Halt, on the Southall-Brentford line. This short-lived station was across the canal from Hanwell; houses in the Boston Road area can be seen in the background.

80. *Ealing Common Station*, Uxbridge Road, *c*1910.

81. Housing contrasts 1: Middle-class housing north of the railway viewed from Ealing Town Hall in 1903. Haven Green Baptist church is to the right of the picture.

More Developments

STOP AND GO

Building houses was and still is a cyclical business, usually depending on large scale economic and market forces. But these factors can sometimes be modified by local ones. Demand can be cultivated by the availability of land, or it can be depressed by the absence of mains drainage or good transport facilities. Market conditions can cause miscalculations so that too many houses are built. In the decade of the 1860s the number of inhabitants in Ealing had risen by 91% and the total of houses by 87%, but in 1871 a sizeable number of those houses were uninhabited. This suggests that supply had outrun demand, and the following decade was one of a slowing down in population growth to 58% and in the number of houses built to 52%. This decennial figure masks the upsurge of activity that took place from 1878 and which was sustained into the early 1880s, peaking in 1883 when plans for 253 new houses were approved. There was then another peak of activity at the end of the century.

Things were different in Hanwell where the growth was only about 55% each decade. But in the 1890s the increase in buildings completed rose to 73%, the sort of increase still being maintained by about 1911. It was only in the 1890s, also, that Hanwell's population showed substantial growth, keeping pace with the house building.

THE WOOD ESTATE

It seems likely that the MDR's plans for a new branch to Ealing and the new suburban service offered by the GWR in the late 1870s were a stimulus. In the 1880s the major development in Ealing was taking place on the Wood estate. The Wood family, with substantial interests in the London coal trade, arrived in Ealing in the late eighteenth century and built up an estate, particularly in the northeast of the parish and across the boundary into Acton. By the 1840s the estate comprised some 900 acres in Ealing and Acton, and George Wood, residing at Hanger Hill House, was the largest landowner in Ealing with 502 acres. He was a prominent and active resident and a short-lived member of the first Local Board, elected in 1863. When he died in 1864 his son, Edward, inherited the property.

Edward Wood moved out to Shropshire and in 1874 Hanger Hill House was let to Edward Monta-

82. Housing contrasts 2: Working-class terraces viewed from the Autotype works, West Ealing in 1903, looking east

gue Nelson, the leading political figure in Ealing, and chairman of the Local Board. The construction of the District Railway across the Wood estate stimulated housing development. At about the same time the area north of the GWR line came under the jurisdiction of the Local Board and high up on the Board's priorities was the provision of mains drainage for this newly-included area.

In Edward Wood's absence the estate was administered from the Hanger Hill estate office in the Broadway by Hugh Robert Hughes, a solicitor; the architectural and technical side of development was handled by Robert Willey, an architect, who was also involved in local affairs – he became mayor in 1906.

Plans for new roads north of Haven Green were approved in 1878. Some plots were freehold, but most were on long leasehold, with a ground rent to the Wood estate. The scheme was developed in an overall style dictated by the estate office and to standards now regulated by bye-laws. Many street names reflected Wood family names, such as Woodville, Boileau and Hamilton, and others were a reminder of the family's Shropshire connections,

such as Corfton, Madeley, and Culmington.

By 1906, when Edward Wood's son sold the estate to the Prudential Assurance for nearly £250,000 over 850 houses had been erected in more than thirty roads, bringing in an annual rental of nearly £8,000. But the building process had been a long one and some roads had taken two decades to complete.

83. The elegant streets north of Haven Green *c*1906. The extensive tree-planting is evident. The building beside the railway containing the stables of Reading & Sons, Jobmasters, still survives.

84. Houses in *Mount Park Crescent*, typical of roads on the Wood Estate in 1902.

OTHER DEVELOPMENTS

No other estate operated on the same scale, although the Mount Park estate had an office at 39 Oxford Road, the home of James Savage, architect and surveyor.

Austin's land was still being developed – Albany, Arlington and Waldeck Roads were completed by the mid 1890s. The major estate to the west of the parish was owned by the Millard family. Building had begun here in the 1860s though most occurred much later; plots were sold freehold, and the houses were more modest than those on the Wood estate, indicating the lower social status of West Ealing. But even here the builders were bound by restrictive covenants which determined the cost and style of their houses.

In the south of the parish serious development began in the late 1870s. The Beaconsfield estate, just south of the church, was being built in 1877 and in 1880 the MDR opened its station at South Ealing. Work began on the Ealing Park estate in 1886, on Murray, Carlisle and Darwin Roads, but Ealing Park House itself survived and became a convent. This estate was noted in 1894 as being chiefly occupied by clerks.

In Hanwell most of the development towards the end of the 19th century was south of the Uxbridge Road, bounded by Boston Road and the Brent river. North of the Uxbridge Road the area was still virtually untouched, although Golden Manor was developed in the 1880s with a series of large houses. Building began on the Hanwell Park estate after 1884 (Framfield and Shakespeare Roads) and more

took place before the First World War.

In 1880 the Ealing, Acton and Hanwell Permanent Benefit Building Society was formed, which had a number of influential local people as directors. These included William Nye, a local builder, and Charles Jones, surveyor to the Local Board. A second building society, the Ealing, Hanwell & District 625th Starr-Bowkett Building Society was formed in the 1880s to appeal to purchasers of more modest means.

Rural Ealing and Hanwell survived in their northern parts. There, people could look out over the Brent valley to Greenford and Perivale, both villages still, and beyond to Horsenden Hill. Some farms lasted into the twentieth century: Pitshanger Farm, sold in 1910, and Brentside Farm, part of which survives as a sports field.

Ealing still was, according to one commentator, 'pleasantly situated amidst charming rusticity, having no spot within its boundaries from which the eye cannot light on refreshing foliage or verdure; and possessing withal every advantage of modern civilisation to the full...an ideal residence for him whom the ceaseless clatter of a mighty city wearies, but on whom at the same time unrelieved monotony of country life pure and simple palls'. Residents seem to have had the best of both worlds, but the fine balance between urban sophistication and rural surroundings was always at risk with continued development. Before the First World War the balance was about right and this is the period when Ealing was labelled 'Queen of the Suburbs'.

85. The surviving countryside at Cotching's Farm, Hanger Lane, *c*1900.

86. The surviving countryside at *Pitshanger Farm*, in 1903.

87. The broad sweep of *Mattock Lane*, looking west towards St John's church, 1892.

88. *St Mary's church, Hanwell.* The new church designed by Gilbert Scott and W.B. Moffatt in 1842.

Hanwell and Ealing at Prayer

Victorian church-going was nowhere near as all-pervasive as it is sometimes portrayed – it was more frequent in middle-class than working-class areas. The increased population in places such as Ealing and Hanwell encouraged a vigorous building programme. At the same time churches built in the classical style in the 18th century were vulnerable to the trend towards Gothic architecture.

The architect Sir Gilbert Scott provides a link between Ealing and Hanwell: he designed a church in each parish. He built St Mary's Hanwell in 1841–42 to replace the austere classical building of 1782 which, despite the addition of a gallery in 1823, became inadequate for the larger congregation. It was one of Scott's earliest commissions, designed in association with W.B. Moffatt, in an Early English style of flint with stone and white brick dressings. The tower at the south-west corner is surmounted by a broach spire.

In Ealing, Scott built Christchurch (now called Christ the Saviour) in the Uxbridge Road, on the corner with Spring Bridge Road, in 1850–52. This church marked the first sub-division of the ancient parish of St Mary's, and was visible confirmation that the centre of Ealing was shifting to the Uxbridge Road – a likely, but not inevitable, consequence of the opening of the GWR station at Haven Green.

The church itself was a private benefaction, paid for by Miss Rosa Lewis in memory of her father, and erected on a site provided by George Wood. With its tall spire and prominent position it became a familiar landmark. The vicarage, which stood to its west, was also designed by Scott, but was demolished to make way for shops in 1930.

Unlike its Hanwell counterpart, the Georgian church of St Mary was retained, but remodelled almost out of recognition by the architect S.S. Teulon between 1865 and 1873. This work involved raising the roof, adding tracery and stained glass to the windows, and attaching buttresses to produce a Venetian Gothic style. This florid detail, and a heavy use of polychrome brickwork, cannot disguise the rather square proportions of the nave.

In the new districts a church was desirable in each of them to add respectability. A familiar pattern emerged in such cases; first, a temporary church would be provided, and then fund-raising would begin for a permanent building. The usual round of fetes, bazaars and concerts would follow: the local paper carried many advertisements and reports of such events.

The church of St John in West Ealing was built in 1876 by E.H. Horne – its steeple was lost in a fire in 1920, and is now replaced by a tower. St Stephen's at the top of the Avenue was built the same year of ragstone with ashlar dressings, the work of J. Ashdown with tower and spire added later by Arthur Blomfield; this served the Austin estate development. Unsafe by the 1970s, it was converted into flats and the congregation transferred to the church hall across the road.

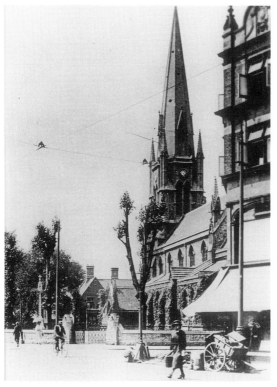

89. *Christchurch, Uxbridge Road*, from the corner of Spring Bridge Road *c*1901. Eldred Sayer's store is on the left, the vicarage demolished in the 1930s, is beside the church.

St Matthew's, North Common Road, began life as a temporary iron church in 1872, and was rebuilt in 1884 to a design by Alfred Jowers. St Peter's in Mount Park Road is architecturally the most distinguished of Ealing's churches. Again originating as an iron church in 1882 to serve this expensive part of North Ealing, it was built anew by J. D. Sedding until his death in 1891 and seen through to consecration by his assistant, Henry Wilson. It is built in yellow brick and Box stone in the decorated style, but with arts and crafts overtones; its chief glory is the massive window at the west end.

Hanwell, unlike Ealing, remained a single parish until the twentieth century, though another church, St Mark's, was built to serve that area south of the Uxbridge Road. This was designed by the distinguished ecclesiastical architect, William White, in the decorated style in brown and red brick.

This part of Middlesex was not notable for a non-conformist tradition – it tended to be church rather than chapel. Hanwell had a dissenters' chapel at the junction of Boston and Lower Boston Roads in the 1820s. Its precise affiliation is unclear but may have been Methodist, but when a new building was opened in Westminster Road in 1869 it was registered as a Baptist and Congregational Union church. But a new Methodist church was built in 1884 in Lower Boston Road, a building taken over in

90. *St Mary's church, Ealing*, as remodelled by S.S. Teulon. Despite the Gothic detail the proportions of the Georgian church are apparent.

91. *St Peter's church, Mount Park Road.*

92. *St Mary's church, Ealing.* The highly decorated interior with its unusual gallery.

1905 by the Salvation Army – the Methodists had, by then, a new church in Church Road.

Ealing had quite a number of non-conformist chapels and churches, although Brentford, with its longer urban history, had a longer dissenting tradition. John Wesley visited Brentford several times in the 1740s. In Ealing proper the earliest Congregational group met in a cottage about 1800, and the first of their chapels to open was in the Grove in 1822. A new chapel, one of Charles Jones's earliest designs, was opened on Ealing Green in 1860. The two Baptist chapels provde a contrast in styles: the West Ealing chapel (1865) is in a classical style, while the Haven Green Baptist Church (1880) was built in an elegant French Gothic manner.

Of the Methodist chapels the most imposing was that built in 1869 on the corner of Windsor Road and Uxbridge Road. A large Presbyterian church, St Andrew, built in 1880, is close to St Peter's in Mount Park Road.

The church militant was concentrated in the working class district behind the High Street; both the Salvation Army and the Blue Ribbon Gospel Army had barracks in Bakers Lane.

Although there was a Roman Catholic mission in Hanwell from 1853 and a permanent church in the Uxbridge Road from 1864, it was only in the 1890s that a mission opened in Ealing. Father O'Halloran had a church in Mattock Lane, where the Questors Theatre is now, and the Benedictines established what is now Ealing Abbey in 1899.

93. The iron church used by the Catholic church of St Joseph and St Peter, Mattock Lane. The building later had a secular use.

94. *The Catholic church of Our Lady & St Joseph*, Hanwell *c*1904.

95. *St Andrew's Presbyterian church*, Mount Park Road.

Municipal Progress and Civic Pride

A LOCAL BOARD

The origins of modern local government lie in the mid-Victorian period, when impetus for administrative change came from the need to improve public health in the crowded towns and cities. The old administrative system based on the parish and the local justices was under strain, particularly in the matter of poor relief where the cost of alleviating poverty had risen dramatically in the early nineteenth century. In Ealing the workhouse, which had space for 142 inmates, was badly overcrowded in 1797: it was 'a small inconvenient building, very ill-adapted to the purpose for which it is applied. When the house is full, four men sleep in a bed: at present 3 men sleep in a bed; four boys in a bed; and 3 women in a bed'. Nearly £3,000 was disbursed in poor relief in 1796–6, both in the upkeep of the workhouse and in pension and relief payments to people in their own houses.

The government's response to the problems of the parishes was to change the system. By the Poor Law Amendment Act of 1834 responsibility for poor relief was transferred to Poor Law Unions. Both Ealing and Hanwell were part of the Brentford Union, which built a new workhouse in Isleworth, leaving the Ealing workhouse to be sold off in 1839.

As regards general parish administration, New Brentford had been separate from Hanwell from the seventeenth century. Ealing was divided into two parts – the 'upper' side, comprising Ealing village and the area northwards, and the 'lower' side, mainly Brentford. The two parts were very different, with Brentford urban and industrial, and the larger in terms of population, while Ealing proper was rural. By the mid-nineteenth century the position was rather different, with Brentford a declining centre, and Ealing poised to develop as a residential suburb.

96. *South Ealing* as seen from the Southern Sewage Works *c*1910.

It was specifically the issue of public health which prompted another important legislative change. The Public Health Act of 1848 established local boards of health to undertake sanitary improvements. Originally it was thought that a single board could serve both Ealing and Brentford, but there was a conflict of interests between upper and lower sides, and so Ealing in 1863 became a separate district.'The feeling locally in those days,' wrote local surveyor Charles Jones, 'was that Brentford, with its much larger population, overwhelmed the voting power of Ealing and prevented the growth of the place'.

The jurisdiction of the Ealing Local Board did not correspond with the area of the historic parish. Not only, of course, did it exclude Brentford in the south, but also the thinly-populated area north of the Great Western railway line. The Board had nine elected members and two paid officials: Charles Jones who was to be its surveyor, architect and engineer for fifty years, and a clerk, Alexander Hemsley, who was also a solicitor and handled the legal business. Not only could the Board improve sanitation, it could arrange water supplies, maintain burial grounds, regulate offensive trades and, later on, manage roads.

97. *Charles Jones*, Ealing's first Surveyor, Architect and Engineer.

98. Mending the roads in 1893. The precise location is unknown.

99. *Ealing Cottage Hospital* in 1873.

100. *Edward Montague Nelson,* chairman of Ealing Local Board.

101. The first Ealing Council offices in The Mall, 1901. The building was occupied by the London and County Bank after the erection of the Town Hall.

The main problem which faced the Board was the inadequate sewage and drainage system. Jones was 'instructed to prepare a scheme which should not only meet the necessities of the moment, but in accordance with his strongly-held view, provide for a largely-increased future'. It will be seen here that the Board accepted that the growth and development of Ealing went hand in hand with a satisfactory infrastructure. The sewage and drainage works proposed required an outlay of £22,000 at a time when the rateable value of the area was less than £20,000. A sewage works was constructed near South Ealing Road; the new drainage system took advantage of the natural fall of the land towards the Thames. These works were said by Jones – not a modest man – to have been quite advanced for the time. Jones, incidentally, introduced into Ealing, a refuse destructor, an idea used earlier in Leeds. This had two functions. One was the combustion of household refuse, the other was the destruction of sewage sludge. Previously the sludge had been sold as manure to farmers, but as the area became less agricultural a new use for it was needed. The destructor turned it into a hard clinker which could be used in road making; or, ground up as a building material, it could even be formed into paving slabs.

Control of the roads was assumed in 1874 and at the same time the Board's jurisdiction was extended north of the railway line to the parish boundary. It was noted at the time that 'houses of a superior class are rapidly extending about Castlebar and Hanger Hill, and the question of a sewage outfall must shortly be raised...' At about this time Brentford was made a separate local board in which Old Brentford and New Brentford were united.

Ealing Local Board could now tackle the urgent sewage problem of north Ealing. Because of the lie of the land parts of the area could not be connected to the existing sewage system and so a second sewage works, on 22 acres by the Brent, was built, large enough to cope with an anticipated population of 15,000 (it was then 2,000).

As part of its responsibilities for the health of the population, the Local Board in 1871 established a cottage hospital at Minton Lodge, West Ealing, and a separate 18-bed isolation hospital in South Ealing Road in 1885. The cottage hospital was enlarged several times before being replaced by the King Edward Memorial Hospital in nearby Mattock Lane in 1911.

The Board's early meetings were at Cross House, where the vestry had met, while their surveyor had his office above a barber's shop in the High Street, but once the Board began to expand and control its own labour force larger premises were needed. New offices, designed by Jones, were built next to the Feathers Hotel on the Uxbridge Road.

A NEW TOWN HALL

The Town Hall and its associated buildings, built in the mid 1880s, superseded the old offices and, at the same time, expressed the civic pride now appropriate to the suburb. This complex included a baths, public library, a fire station, stabling and workshops, as well as the town hall. The baths included three pools for men and one for women, one of them convertible to use as a badminton court or gymnasium.

Jones designed the Town Hall itself, in his characteristic, but perhaps by now rather dated, Gothic style, at a cost of £16,000. The fire station was behind by the railway line, complete with watchtower and stables. The adjacent Victoria Hall was provided by public subscription, although the trusteeship was vested in the Board. This was modelled on a medieval baronial hall and was designed to be the major function room of the parish, with the profits from lettings given to charitable causes. Of the subscribers to this, Edward Montague Nelson, chairman of the Board, Edward Wood and Baron Rothschild, the owner of Gunnersbury Park, each gave £500, and the remainder was raised by the issue of £10 debentures. On 15 December 1889 the Prince of Wales opened the Victoria Hall with appropriate pomp and entertainment.

102. *Ealing Town Hall.*

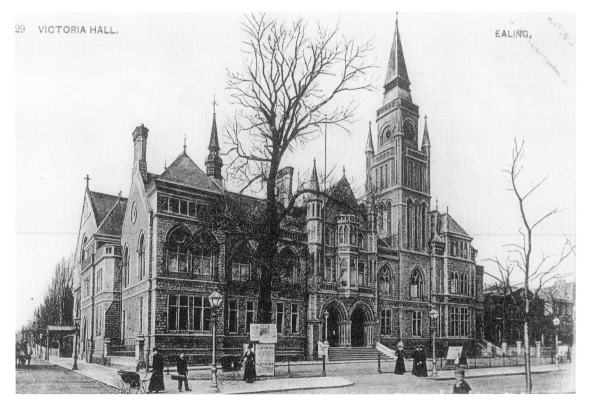

103. Cartoon celebrating the opening of the Victoria Hall, Ealing, by the Prince of Wales in 1888.

104. *Ealing Baths*. One of the baths could be converted for use as a gymnasium.

105. The interior of the *Victoria Hall*, Ealing Town Hall.

SUPPLYING THE PUBLIC

As in the rest of London, gas supply was in the control of private companies. In Ealing's case the supplier by 1846 was the Brentford Gas Company. But by the time that electrical supply was feasible there was a trend for local authorities, unhappy with the way the gas companies had performed, to attempt to supply electricity themselves. Generators were installed in South Ealing for both street lighting and domestic users, and by the end of 1894 was fully operational; by 1902 over 1000 customers were connected. One of the early, handsome street lamp standards still survives at the junction of Woodville and Aston roads.

The supply of water continued under private control. In Ealing it was supplied by the Grand Junction Waterworks Company, though not very satisfactorily it seems, for a government report of 1879 listing 241 urban districts without a proper piped supply, includes Ealing. This was, presumably, remedied by the construction of the Fox Reservoir on Hanger Hill in 1888.

106. *The opening of the Fox Reservoir* on 3 August 1888. The reservoir was named after Edwin G. Fox, chairman of the Grand Junction Waterworks Company, who performed the opening ceremony.

107. *The water tower, Fox Reservoir*, Hanger Hill, 1902. The tower, on the crest of the hill, is visible for some distance.

PROGRESS IN HANWELL

The establishment of a Local Board occurred much later in Hanwell. For the purposes of sanitary arrangements and building regulations Hanwell had previously been joined with Greenford, Perivale and Twyford in a rural sanitary authority, an agency of the Brentford Poor Law Union.

Agitation for Hanwell to be independent in these matters was successful in 1885. In the case to the government's inspector it was claimed that 'Hanwell was no longer a rural parish. People from town came to reside in the place, as the population was still rapidly increasing, they thought it only fair that the ratepayers should be able to improve their position in a sanitary point of view, and control the expenditure of those who were in office...There were no adequate bye-laws to govern the laying out of land and the erection of houses.'

The small Hanwell Local Board (only nine members in 1885) had no specific meeting place until 1891 when it purchased Cherington House. Its functions were much the same as Ealing's – the modernisation of the sewage system, drainage and so on, but it gradually took on extra work such as parks and libraries. A Carnegie public library was opened next to Cherington House in 1905.

Both Ealing and Hanwell became Urban District Councils in 1895, but Ealing, created a borough in 1901, absorbed Hanwell, Greenford and Perivale in 1926 and Northolt in 1928.

108. *Cherington House*, Hanwell, the offices of Hanwell Urban District Council.

109. Guests assembled on Ealing Common on 10 July 1901 for the reading of the Charter of Incorporation, by which Ealing achieved borough status.

Schools for the Masses

CHARITY SCHOOLS

Alongside the private schools for middle-class children were charitable schools for the poorer classes.

A boys' school attached to St Mary's, Ealing, was operating by 1714; new and larger premises were built in 1719 and 1782. The school was supported by subscriptions, sermons, and some legacies, notably those of Lady Capel (d1711), Jonathan Gurnell snr and jnr, James Taylor and Mrs Alithia Stafford. In the early nineteenth century these benefactions, providing an income of £60 per annum, enabled twenty boys to be clothed and taught to read, write and, as Lysons puts it, 'to cast accounts'. The master of the school, who had a house and garden attached, was paid £40 a year.

Jane Rawlinson, who died in 1712, left £500 to clothe and educate twenty girls, but there was no separate school for girls until the end of the eighteenth century when thirteen acres of land near the church were bought to endow a school: it was erected in 1795 on the west side of Ealing Green.

There is no record of systematic charitable education in Hanwell before 1780. Children could then attend the school begun in Greenford by the rector of that parish, Edward Betham. Also, the trustees of Hobbayne's Charity began using part of their income to pay the school fees of a few poor children, who probably attended a school in Brentford. The trustees then decided to fund a school in Hanwell. Samuel Glasse, rector of the parish, bought and equipped a house near the church and it was opened with 24 pupils in 1782. It was not a substantial building evidently for it was blown down in a gale in 1800. Rebuilt on the same site by Glasse's son, the building was later known as Rectory Cottage. A further new building in Half Acre Road was opened in 1807.

Education was also provided by the Sunday school movement. Such schools had started in Ealing in 1786 with the encouragement and attention of Sarah Trimmer, a well-known and influential proponent of moral and religious education, who lived in Brentford. By the early nineteenth century, Lysons tells us, 'about sixty boys and more than a hundred girls are now educating in the Sunday schools of this parish, which are conducted upon a plan which affords great encouragement to the meritorious, and seems admirably calculated to excite a spirit of emulation and improvement.'

110. *Hanwell Parish School.*

NATIONAL AND BRITISH SCHOOLS

The changes in society produced by the Industrial Revolution increased demand for education for all classes. The National Society for Promoting the Education of the Poor in the Principles of the Established Church, founded in 1811, became by far the largest purveyor of education to the poorer classes until the establishment by the government of elementary schools. As will be seen from the Society's title, education was strictly on Anglican lines and, generally, the schools were attached to churches. Its rival was the British and Foreign School Society, founded in 1814, committed to education which included non-denominational religious teaching.

By the early 1840s the National school in Hanwell had 66 boys and 45 girls attending, out of a total of 207 children at all the elementary schools in the parish. The other establishments included four Dame schools charging 3d to 6d per week, three of which were kept by non-conformists, the fourth by an Anglican. The common day school (a private school) charged between 13s and 21s a quarter, depending on the amount of instruction the pupil

received, but the curriculum was limited to reading, writing, arithmetic, history and geography.

There were thirteen schools in Ealing with a total of 339 pupils. Of these 159 children attended the National school where, it is said, the only book available was the Bible. While the boys were taught reading, writing, arithmetic, grammar and the outlines of geography and history, the girls were restricted to reading, writing and a little arithmetic and scripture.

The girls' National school building on Ealing Green was rebuilt in 1862 (it is now used by Jehovah's Witnesses) and the boys' school in South Ealing Road added to in 1874. As new parishes were formed so National schools were attached to the new churches.

The only British School in Ealing appears to have been that opened in 1859, in Lancaster Road, behind the High Street; though it charged high fees it had a good reputation and over 200 pupils were attending in the 1870s. A Wesleyan school next to the Methodist church in Windsor Road in 1874 was also more expensive and attracted middle-class children.

111. *Hanwell National School* (St Mark's) in 1855.

112. *The Wesleyan School*, beside the Methodist church, The Mall, Ealing, *c*1901.

113. Miss Cumming's class at the Wesleyan School *c*1917.

114. *Lady Noel Byron.*

LADY BYRON'S SCHOOL

In Ealing there were six Dame schools, all of them Anglican, and two common day schools, one of which was the celebrated school founded by Lady Byron, the widow of the poet. She was interested in a system of education for working class children that combined elementary learning with the acquisition of practical skills, and she was particularly influenced by the innovatory methods of the Swiss de Fellenberg, whom she had visited at Hofwyl in 1828. Her school was established in 1834 at Ealing Grove House, a mansion to the east side of the Green. Day boys from six years old were charged 2d per week, and there were boarders, from the age of twelve, at £14 per annum. In the early 1840s there were 48 boarders and 24 day scholars.

The curriculum here included, apart from the basic subjects, geology and agricultural chemistry, drawing and carpentry. In contrast to the use of the monitorial system at National schools, every effort was made at Ealing Grove to use modern educational methods, and a wide variety of apparatus was available, including maps, globes, models and diagrams. Corporal punishment was not used. Gardening was an integral part of the regime: each boy was given a plot and expected to work it, partly to benefit the school and partly on his own account. Other skills such as measuring, geometry and accounting were taught through the management of his garden.

Tremenheere, an enthusiastic investigator, found that 'in addition to a reasonable and useful amount of general instruction, some practical skill had been acquired from the handicraft and garden work, and habits of active industry formed, amidst much cheerfulness and content, and feelings of confidence and attachment to their masters, and of kindliness to each other.' The school later evolved into a private high school, after Lady Byron relinquished control to Charles Atlee.

STATE EDUCATION

Forster's famous Education Act of 1870, establishing elementary education, had little impact in Ealing and Hanwell. The Act enabled, but didn't oblige, local authorities to set up schools, funded by the rates, if they thought that existing provision was inadequate. But Ealing and Hanwell parishes declined to adopt the Act: the only pressure to do so came from non-conformists who resented the dominance of the National Society in the area. However, by the end of the century both National and British schools were overcrowded and it was at last conceded that a School Board should be established and new buildings erected.

But there had been an intermediate phase in Ealing. In 1877 the Ealing Educational Association had been set up. This levied voluntary subscriptions and used them to support the existing schools and to fund capital projects. Although avowedly non-denominational it was regarded as being Anglican in character. But despite its efforts such voluntary assistance could not keep pace with the relentless rise in the school population – from 754 in 1878 to 2388 in 1902. In that latter year Balfour's Education Act abolished school boards and replaced them with local education authorities; Ealing Borough Council, as it had become by then, finally assumed responsibility for elementary education, with secondary education going to the county.

Ealing built its first schools to the designs of Charles Jones – Little Ealing, Northfields (both 1905), Drayton Grove (1908), Lammas (1910), and North Ealing (1911).

Saving the Countryside

Battles to save open space in the London, such as those that had already taken place over Hampstead Heath and Wimbledon Common, inspired the passing of the Metropolitan Commons Act of 1866. This provided for commons within the Metropolitan Police District to be preserved for the public. By then Ealing and Hanwell had lost many of their fields and open spaces; taking advantage of this new Act Ealing Local Board sought to take over responsibility for Ealing Common and, eventually, other smaller pieces of common land in the district. In this way the Board purchased Ealing Common, Haven Green and Ealing Green for a nominal £500 and later Drayton Green was added for £1000.

These spaces were all in the north of the district. In the area between St Mary's and West Ealing the Board bought thirty acres of Lammas land for £4000 – the name derives from the medieval right of manorial tenants to graze their cattle on the stubble left after a harvest, as from Lammas Day, 1 August. On this land the Board created Lammas Park, opened with ceremony in 1883, appropriately on 1 August,

116. Taking a promenade on Ealing Common, *c*1900.

115. Ponds on the north side of Ealing common; the houses are in North Common Road.

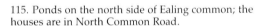

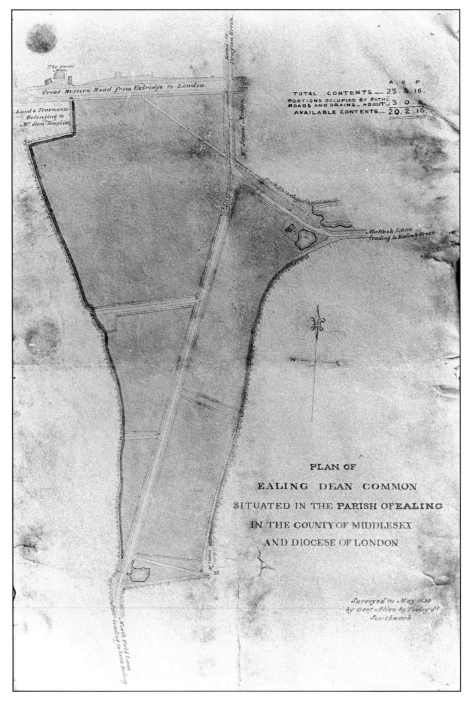

The Green
Inn

Great Western Road from Uxbridge to London

Land & Tenements
Belonging to
Mr Sam Tompkins

Road to
Drayton Green

Mr Samuel Mason

A. R. P.

TOTAL CONTENTS — 23. 2. 16.
PORTIONS OCCUPIED BY PATHS
ROADS AND DRAINS — ABOUT — 3. 0. 9.
AVAILABLE CONTENTS — 20. 2. 16

Matlock Lane
leading to Ealing Green

PLAN OF

EALING DEAN COMMON

SITUATED IN THE PARISH OF EALING

IN THE COUNTY OF MIDDLESEX

AND DIOCESE OF LONDON

Surveyed in May 1832
by Geo! Allen by Tooley S!
Southwark

North Field Lane
leading to Little Ealing

117. *A Plan of Ealing Dean Common*, 1832, when the common was divided into allotments for the poor. Northfield Lane is the road running down the map.

118. *Lammas Park* after twenty years of municipal care, *c*1900.

119. *A view of Walpole Park* from Pitshanger Manor, 1903.

and though the ground was meant for recreation, cows were still being grazed there at the time.

But the 'jewel in the crown' was undoubtedly Walpole Park. This park, more than thirty acres, came into public ownership in 1900 and together with Lammas Park, which it adjoins, forms a green corridor through residential south Ealing. The land was originally the grounds of Pitshanger Manor, the home in the eighteenth century of the Gurnell family, and the property for much of the nineteenth of Spencer Walpole MP. A distinguished politician in his own right, he had married the daughter of the former prime minister, Spencer Perceval (see p. 24). Included in the grounds were some fine old trees, including a pair of Cedars of Lebanon, planted at the beginning of the nineteenth century.

Although the purchase (for £40,000) of both house and grounds had actually taken place early in 1900 (the Middlesex County Council had contributed £10,000), Ealing had to wait until three months after the death of the last of its residents, Frederika Perceval, in May 1900 to take full possession. The park was opened in 1901 and the public library in the house followed the next year. In 1984 Pitshanger Museum took the place of the library here.

Other open spaces include Pitshanger Park, about 26 acres, and Hanger Hill park, five acres, which were added before the First World War. But another type of open space was owned by Ealing much earlier. This consisted of allotments near St Mary's church, provided by a charity established by Lady Rawlinson, and another set in West Ealing, given in 1832 for the use of the poor by the Bishop of London, Lord of the Manor, comprising some twenty acres of waste. In 1840 there were 146 allotments here each let at a yearly rent of five shillings. It was reported that by good cultivation such an allotment could yield twenty sacks of potatoes, which would provide for a labourer's family and provide a small surplus for sale.

Hanwell retained a much smaller amount of open space. The parish had been enclosed by statute in 1816 and at that time only about 1¼ acres had been set aside on the heath for the poor to compensate for the loss of common rights – this space later became King George's Fields. Churchfields, surrounding the church and overlooking the Brent, was bought in 1898 for the public, but at the time Hanwell was merged with Ealing in 1926 only some 34 acres of public open space were available.

120. *Haven Green c*1905.

121. *Pitshanger Manor, Walpole Park*, in use as a public library.

122. *Rus in urbe* – cows graze near Hanwell Church. Churchfields became a public park in 1898.

Trade and Industry

AN INDUSTRIAL BAN

Unlike neighbouring areas of West Middlesex such as Acton, Brentford and Southall, neither Ealing nor Hanwell became industrial centres. In Ealing the Local Board was able to exclude industry almost entirely, though in the period after World War II a commercial area developed, especially as offices replaced houses along the Uxbridge Road between the Broadway and West Ealing. The small amount of industry was concentrated in West Ealing: the Autotype Company, a printing works, was in Brownlow Road, the Albion Alumenizing Company, which made coated papers, was in Bloomfield Road; the soft drinks factory of Hilton and Company was in St Mary's Road. Ottway & Company, optical instrument makers, had workshops in New Broadway and Wolf Electric Tools became a major employer when they opened their Pioneer Works in Hanger Lane in 1935.

In 1901 the largest employment sector for men was the building trade although, of course, large numbers of residents commuted into the City and the West End.

SERVANTS AND LAUNDRIES

For women the main occupation was domestic service – there were, at that time, 68 servants to each one hundred households. This can be compared with sixteen in Hanwell and 23 in London overall. There were several employment agencies specifically for servants in Ealing. Thomas Carey, of 30 The Broadway, combined a greengrocery business with a registry office for domestics; in 1894 Augustus West was operating the Helena Domestic Agency near Ealing Broadway station.

This plenitude of servants in Ealing produced a wide imbalance in the population – there were, in 1911, 29,777 women and only 19,812 men. Of the women, 6,590 were engaged in domestic service or the related occupations of charing or laundry work.

Acton, nicknamed 'Soapsud Island', was the centre of the west London laundry industry, taking in washing from the inner suburbs. Hanwell's part in this industry was at first small-scale, concentrated in the narrow streets between Boston Road and the canal. A Hanwell resident remembered her mother working at 'a little laundry down our road' from eight in the morning to nine at night. Large-scale firms developed – the Ealing District Steam Laundry beside Northfields station, and the Troy Laundry in West Ealing. In the 1890s dry cleaners began to compete – Eastman's had a receiving office in Ealing and their works in Acton Vale.

Hanwell had some light engineering firms by the canals. In the 1890s, in addition to the laundries, there was a 'pewterer and beer-engine maker', and also the works of W.E. Hill & Sons, the celebrated violin makers.

THE
Troy Laundry Coy.
WEST EALING,

— For —
BEST WORK
— at —
Moderate Prices.

BY the closest attention to details, the use of the best selected soaps we can buy, an abundance of pure water, and good open-air drying grounds, we have won a reputation for good work that is second to none.

FLANNELS WASHED IN DISTILLED WATER.

Glossy Satin Finish to Table Linen.

SHIRTS, COLLARS AND CUFFS BEAUTIFULLY FINISHED.

Window and Furniture Draperies carefully Cleaned.

123. *The Troy Laundry Company*, West Ealing. An advertisement in the *Ealing and Hanwell Year Book* 1907.

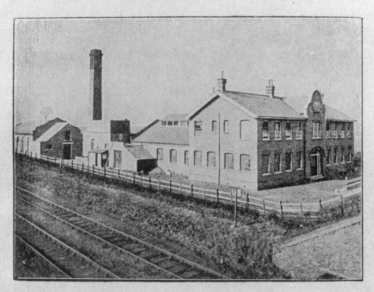

124. *The Ealing District Steam Laundry.* An advertisement in the *Ealing and Hanwell Year Book* 1908.

The Local Shops

THE VILLAGE STORES

Great claims were made for Ealing shops at the end of the century. In the 1890s a journalist wrote in *Ealing Illustrated*: 'Undaunted by, but not unmindful of, the, from their point of view, somewhat perilous proximity of the gigantic metropolis, Ealing tradesmen have resolved that as far as they are concerned, the town shall be thoroughly self-supporting, and there is not a residential centre in England where greater facilities for purchasing goods of every conceivable description, up-to-date in every respect and cheap withal, obtain'.

It is difficult to judge the validity of such claims. It is also difficult to pinpoint the moment at which the Ealing shopping centre was created. When Ealing was not much more than a village the tradesmen were those typical of a rural community – four bakers, five butchers, fourteen grocers and, in 1839, three blacksmiths, two wheelwrights, two saddlers and two corn dealers. Thereafter the nature of the tradesmen reflected the middle-class growth of Ealing. In 1886 there was only one pawnbroker, and that was in West Ealing, but there were seven florists, two music-sellers, eight jewellers and watchmakers, three wine merchants and a cricket-ing outfitter.

The middle-classes shopped in some comfort. Not only were they allowed to run up credit in the shops, but orders were taken at their homes and deliveries made there. The general lack of mechanical refrigeration made speed of distribution important. The Hanger Hill Dairy Farm, which had premises in The Mall and was owned by a Mr Johnson, claimed to deliver milk twice daily within half-an-hour of milking. Mr Sanders of 9, The Parade, Haven Green, fishmonger, poulterer and game dealer, offered to supply fresh salmon, sole, whitebait, turbot and oysters – again, all these could be delivered. Some of the greengrocers were still able to offer vegetables grown on their own land: Thomas Carey, mentioned earlier, had nine acres in Hanwell, including glasshouses.

Other businessmen liked to stress their metropolitan backgrounds. Mr Weaver of 48, the Broadway, claimed that he was not only a perfumer and ornamental hair manufacturer, but a 'court hairdresser' as well (although this term might mean no more than an effort to appear very high class); F.G. Curtis, a chemist, had previously worked at Allen & Hanbury's in Lombard Street and, going one step further, Madame Marie Ellis described herself as an 'artiste in costumes' and indicated a Parisian background.

125. *Ealing Broadway*, from the Feathers Hotel looking west in 1887. The spire of Christchurch is in the background.

126. *Ealing Broadway c1890.* The photograph is taken from the Railway Hotel; Eldred Sayers is on the left, Sanders to the right, on the corner of the High Street.

127. Many shops had delivery services until the last war. Here we see the delivery van of Eden's, a long-established baker and confectioner in Ealing High Street, negotiating Perivale Lane *c*1900 at a time of flooding by the river Brent.

128. *Ealing Broadway c*1910. there have been a number of changes. The electric tram had arrived in 1901, electric light has replaced the gas lamps, and the dome has been added to the corner of the Sayers building.

A CHANGE IN SHOPPING

The second half of the nineteenth century brought two important retailing trends: the growth of department and chain stores. Most department stores grew out of drapery businesses, although a few, notably Harrods, began as grocers. The department store was essentially a response to middle-class shopping requirements, offering a wide range of goods at low prices, but towards the end of the century more emphasis was placed on the attractiveness of the stores and the amenities of shopping in them. In Ealing, both Eldred Sayers and John Sanders expanded from drapery businesses, and their proprietors became men of substance and position.

Sayers occupied a prominent site on the corner of the Uxbridge Road and Spring Bridge Road, a building further adorned by the addition of a dome at the turn of the century. It was claimed that his business was 'Empire-wide': 'Then there were many families, resident in the colonies and India, who making a temporary stay in Ealing now and again, when they return abroad, still continue to deal with Messrs Sayers & Son, and have the necessary supplies of drapery and millinery goods sent out to them as required'. The Sayers store was later acquired by Bentalls.

Across the road from them was John Sanders, his premises occupying a straggling row of buildings between Western Road and the corner of the High Street. By the 1890s he was described as a draper, house furnisher, clothier and outfitter. A similar firm, F.H. Rowse, opened a store in West Ealing, in the Uxbridge Road.

By the 1880s there were 88 firms in Great Britain which had more than ten branches. Most of the early multiples were in footwear, grocery and the meat trades, but there were quite a few branches of W.H. Smith and (in Scotland) John Menzies, and of the Singer sewing machine company. In the mid-1890s Ealing had branches of shoe shops such as Freeman, Hardy & Willis, Lilley & Skinner and Rabbits & Sons, and also the grocers Liptons.

Some businesses were 'local multiples' with shops in both Hanwell and Ealing, among them Gapp Brothers, grocers, and Stevens the butchers. W.B. Hieatt in Ealing Broadway appears to have been the largest provision merchant. He was described as a grocer and cheesemonger, but he also bottled his own beers, blended his own whisky, and made his own aerated water at a factory in West Ealing; at any one time, it was estimated, 2,000 of his soda water siphons were in circulation in the area.

Ealing's shopping centre was concentrated on the Uxbridge Road, High Street and Spring Bridge Road. Many of the shops in the Uxbridge Road were conversions of earlier buildings, where single storey additions were tacked on to houses set back from the road. By the 1880s purpose-built shopping parades had appeared, and early this century Bond Street, a new shopping street, was driven through

129. *Alfred Phillips music shop* in The Mall, 1904.

130. *The Mall, Ealing* in 1890. This new parade with its shutters and elegant lamps, was built in the early 1880s.

the remains of the Ashton House estate, and a parade of shops in the Uxbridge Road, Sandringham Parade, replaced the houses of Sandringham Gardens. On the opposite side of the road a number of houses were demolished to make way for another parade, complete with Dutch gables and a similar group replaced the old almshouses opposite the Feathers Hotel.

By contrast with Ealing Broadway the shops in West Ealing and Hanwell had less pretension and there was greater informality. Though there was no regular street market West Ealing had (and still has) fruit and vegetable stalls. Hanwell had a large group of general shopkeepers, who supplied basic needs to a largely working-class clientele, often from the typical corner shop. The multiples were slower to make an impact here, and there was no department store, though Vaux had a large drapery business in the Uxbridge Road. The weekend shopping could be a social event, as one resident, recalling his youth tells us: 'Saturday nights were really an evening out. You go around Hanwell Broadway and do your shopping Saturday evening late. It was a real trip round to get your cheap meat, listen to the Salvation Army band, playing in the Broadway – they used to play every Saturday night...a real village turn out.'

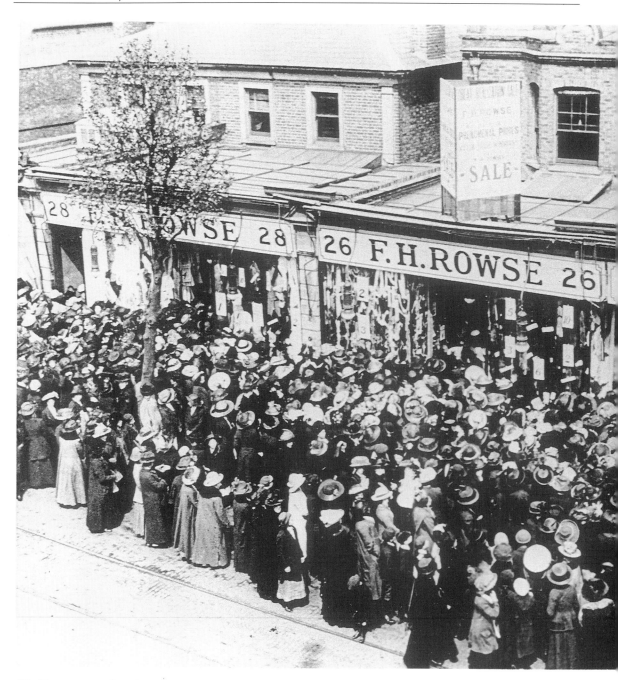

131. Shoppers crowding the pavement outside Rowse's store in West Ealing during its first sale in 1913.

132. *New Broadway, Ealing* in 1904. The new parade of shops between the Town Hall and Christchurch.

133. *Hanwell Broadway*, looking east in 1881. Gapp's Stores are in the centre, the Duke of York public house behind. The Uxbridge Road was very wide at this point.

134. *The High Street, Ealing c*1905, looking towards Eldred Sayers. The building on the left was later occupied by Lamerton's.

135. *Gapp's Stores, 52 The Broadway, Ealing* in 1909. There were branches throughout West London, including one in Hanwell.

136. *The Uxbridge Road, West Ealing c*1905. Mara's china and glass shop stood on the corner of Drayton Green Road, and was replaced by a bank.

137. Vegetable stall at West Ealing in 1911.

138. A corner shop near the Autotype works, West Ealing, 1903.

139. *Blackwell's Dairy, Uxbridge Road, Hanwell*. Delivery men outside the shop *c*1905.

140. *Stowell's Corner*, near West Ealing Station *c*1910. The Drayton Court Hotel in The Avenue is on the right of the picture and one of the elegant municipal lamp standards in the centre.

141. Shops at the bottom of the High Street, facing Ealing Green, *c 1910*.

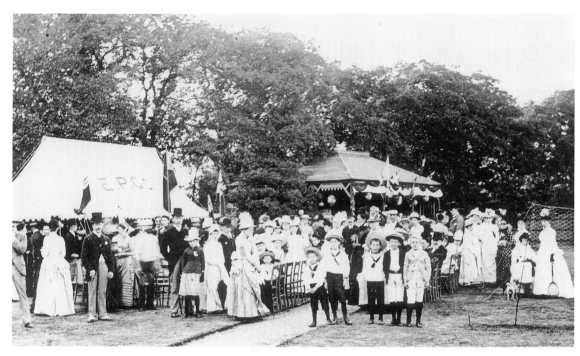

142. *Spectators at Ealing Park Cricket Club.*

The Social Scene

VILLAGE SOCIETY

With the transition from village to suburb there was a shift from an informal society to an organised and institutionalised one. The large range of clubs and societies that are a feature of Ealing at the end of the nineteenth century was a consequence not only of the increase in population but also of the leisure, purchasing power and enthusiasm of the middle classes.

The most prestigious sporting club was the Ealing Cricket Club, with a ground in Woodville Road, described as second-to-none in London, complete with a handsome and commodious pavilion. The club had been formed in 1871 by a group of clergymen, but was not the oldest – Ealing Dean Club had been founded some nine years previously. One of its major social functions of the winter was a ball at the Lyric Hall.

Ealing Lawn Tennis Club, founded in 1882 and originally for archery as well, also had social cachet. Probably the most strangely named club was the Ealing Inanimate Shooting Club, whose ground was in Creffield Road. Many other sports were followed, including the newly introduced game of badmin-

ton. The grounds of Hanger Hill House became a golf course in 1901, while Hanwell had its Brent Valley Club. Cycling became popular in the 1880s if the number of cycle dealers is an indication, and enthusiasts could join the Ealing District Cycling Club.

Clubs and societies reflected a wide range of Victorian enthusiasms, from photography to gardening. The Ealing, Acton and Hanwell Horticultural Society had its first summer show in the grounds of Elm Grove House in 1864 – Spencer Walpole was president for 21 years. Lower down the social scale the Ealing District Gardeners' Mutual Improvement Society seemed to be aimed at the professional gardeners.

Music, both amateur and professional, was popular. A number of choirs and bands flourished, including the celebrated Hanwell Band, formed in 1891, which rehearsed in a room at the Viaduct Inn.

Some organisations had more altruistic aims, notably the Ealing Philanthropic Society, and there were also branches of many national bodies, like the RSPCA. In 1894 a meeting was advertised 'on account of the work being done amongst Acton laundry and factory girls of London'.

Soup kitchens were provided for the poor: the Winter Gift fund raised money for 'the relief of deserving classes in want of help during the winter months' and coal was given at Christmas.

143. *Hanger Hill House* in use as a golf club *c*1905.

144. *Bryant's Tricycle Stand* at Gunnersbury Park *c*1886.

ENTERTAINING THE PEOPLE

The Lyric Hall, in the Broadway, comprised an auditorium, winter garden, picture gallery and terrace. Here, touring companies staged plays and operas. In 1894 Beerbohm Tree's company gave Oscar Wilde's *Woman of no Importance*; other plays, such as the *Silver King*, described in the programme as 'the greatest play of the age', have stood the test of time less well. The theatre was adaptable: the seats in the auditorium could be removed to reveal a polished dance floor. In 1899 it was replaced by the (New) Ealing Theatre, said to be one of the largest theatres in suburban London. The same building incorporated the Lyric Assembly Rooms, which had facilities for dances, bazaars, concerts and amateur theatricals, and were home to many local societies. From 1912 Ealing Cinematograph and a billiard hall used part of the premises and in 1914 the theatre became a fully-fledged cinema, later known as the Palladium. It was demolished in 1958.

Ealing's famous amateur theatre, the Questors, was formed in 1929. Its early productions were staged at the Park Theatre, Hanwell but from 1923 it used an old iron church in Mattock Lane, until this was demolished in 1963 to make way for a purpose built theatre.

As for other cinemas, the Walpole in Bond Street, was converted from a skating rink in 1912; the Kinema, on the site of the old cottage hospital on the corner of Northfield Avenue in 1913, was rebuilt in 1928 and became the Lido. Though much altered it is, since the demise of the Walpole, the oldest cinema in Ealing. The Odeon, Northfields, now a night club, has one of the finest cinema interiors of the 1930s. Designed by Cecil Massey in 1932, it was originally known as the Avenue, but popularly called 'Spanish City' on account of its Moorish external detail and elaborate interior. In contrast the Forum in Uxbridge Road (later the ABC, then a Cannon) was built in 1934 in a quasi-Egyptian style.

Hanwell had two cinemas by 1917, but the Coronation Picture Palace in the Uxbridge Road was shortlived. The Grand, later the Curzon, in Cherington Road, lasted until 1955.

145. From a *Lyric Hall, Ealing* programme. This theatre was the precursor of the Ealing Theatre.

146. *Poster for the Lyric Hall, Ealing* 1894.

147. *Ealing Theatre*, The Broadway, Ealing, c1904.

148. The back of the *Ealing Theatre* from the railway, 1912.

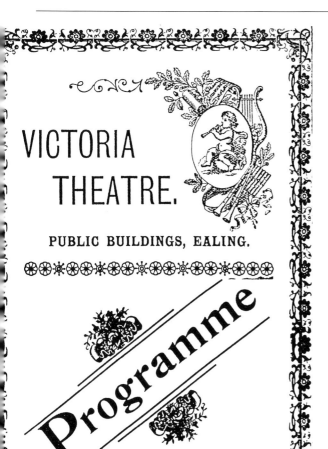

VICTORIA THEATRE.

PUBLIC BUILDINGS, EALING.

Programme

Doors open 7.30.   Commence at 8.

Early Doors to all parts of the Theatre (Grand Entrance), at 7.15, Sixpence Extra.

FAUTEUILS, 3s.   STALLS, 2s.
ADMISSION, 1s.   *(Entrance Longfield Avenue.)*

Schools and Children under 12 years of age, Half-price to Matinees. Children in arms not admitted.

Seats can be booked at Tyer's Library, Broadway, from 10 till 7.

The Management reserve to themselves the right of refusing admission to any person or persons they may think necessary.

Convenient 'Buses and Trains after the Performances to all Parts.

Secretary (for Mr. T. J. PHILLIPS) Mrs. A. A. HUNT.

149. Programme cover for the *Victoria Hall,* part of the Town Hall, Ealing.

VICTORIA HALL.

NOTICE.—*Owing to* MR. BEN. NATHAN'S *inability to fulfil his Contract,* MISS CISSIE LOFTUS WILL NOT APPEAR, *as announced on Feb. 3rd, 4th & 5th.*

MR. T. J. PHILLIPS has much pleasure in announcing that he has been able to arrange, at very short notice, for

MR. CHARLES COLLETTE

TO APPEAR ON
THURSDAY, FRIDAY & SATURDAY, FEB. 3RD, 4TH & 5TH, AT 8.
SPECIAL MATINEE, Saturday, February 5th, at 3.
Schools and Children under 12 Years of Age, HALF-PRICE.

MR. CHARLES COLLETTE,

From the Haymarket, Lyceum, and Principal London Theatres, so long famous for his performance of "THE COLONEL," will give his

DRAMATIC, MIMETIC, MUSICAL, MONOLOGUE, BURLESQUE PATTER ENTERTAINMENT, ENTITLED:

COLLETTE AT HOME,

As recently given by him at Marlborough House before THEIR ROYAL HIGHNESSES THE PRINCE & PRINCESS OF WALES, and a large party of Royal Guests.

Thursday, Friday & Saturday, Feb. 10th, 11th & 12th, at 8, Matinee, Feb. 12th, at 3,

THE LIARS,

TIME & PRICES AS USUAL.   From the Criterion Theatre, London.

SEATS CAN BE BOOKED AT TYER'S LIBRARY, BROADWAY.

150. Advertisement for entertainment at the *Victoria Hall.*

151. *Ealing Theatre* , renamed the Hippodrome in 1912 before becoming the Palladium Cinema.

152. *The first Questors Theatre* premises in an old Catholic church, shortly before demolition in 1958, when the present Questors Theatre was built.

153. *The Walpole Cinema, Bond Street*, shortly before it closed in 1971. Although the cinema was demolished, the fascia was preserved and re-erected in the car park behind.

154. *The interior of the Odeon, Northfields, with its Spanish decoration.*

THE VOLUNTEERS

The Ealing Volunteers, an auxiliary defence force established in 1860 when there was a threat of a French invasion, also had a social role. The company had a drill hall in West Ealing and a rifle range on the meadows by the Brent. It survived, as part of the 2nd Battalion of the Duke of Cambridge's Own Middlesex Regiment, until the formation of the Territorial Army after the Boer War.

KEEPING INFORMED

The present *Ealing Gazette* has its origins in the *Ealing Post & General Advertiser* first issued by J.E. Acworth in 1863. This weekly paper carried news from a wider area, including Hanwell, and was re-named the *Middlesex County Times* in 1868. The paper covered the major events of the day, often in exhaustive detail. The *Times* merged with its rival, the *West Middlesex Gazette*, in 1941.

LOCAL POLITICS

The Conservative Party was the dominant political party in Ealing in the second half of the nineteenth century. It operated two clubs – the Constitutional and the Ealing Dean Conservative Club. The Constitutional, opened in 1890, had premises in the Uxbridge Road in the style of a gentleman's club, with smoking, billiard and reading rooms. The Ealing Dean club, owned by the Constitutional, catered for a more working-class membership.

The Conservatives also promoted themselves in branches – 'habitations' – of the Primrose League, an organisation founded in 1884 to recruit a mass membership for the Conservatives which it did by promoting a social and educational programme and by adopting a masonic style and ritual. The Ealing Habitation was formed in 1885; its 'ruling councillor' was Thomas B. Christie, the superintendent of the Royal India Asylum, and in Hanwell there was a Brent Primrose Club. Many of the leading local politicians and businessmen were members of the Freemasons – the Haven Lodge, No. 2022, was formed in 1884.

155. *Hanwell children at a treat organised by the Brent Habitation of the Primrose League in the grounds of Hanwell Park, to mark the Queen's Jubilee in 1887.*

156. *A fair on Ealing Common c1910.*

THE LOCAL PUBS

In the 1880s there were in Ealing nineteen public houses, some of them survivors from the coaching age, and a further ten beershops, many of which later obtained full licences; one such, the Royal Oak, was said to have been built of bricks from Castle Hill Lodge, the Duke of Kent's house. The railway had its impact on names. The North Star was reputedly named after the early GWR locomotive, and when the proprietor of the Feathers Hotel, the nearest pub to Ealing Broadway station, attempted to incorporate 'Railway' into its name, objections were raised by the licencee of the Railway Hotel, further down the Broadway.

The Feathers, like most of the older inns, was in need of modernisation by the turn of the century; the Old Hats had a very run-down appearance. Most were rebuilt though few with quite the embellishment that the Bell received. Away from the main shopping areas, inns like the Plough, in Little Ealing Lane, kept a rural charm, and could offer patrons a pleasure garden and bowling green. The Fox Inn, in Green Lane, Hanwell was the meeting point for the hunt well into this century.

In an attempt to lure people away from the evils of drink the temperance movement encouraged the opening of coffee houses. By the mid–1890s there was one in Hanwell and several in Ealing; of these the Netherleigh Arms in West Ealing, although a 'coffee-tavern', had the external trappings of a public house.

The licencee of the Feathers built the Drayton Court, adjacent to West Ealing station, in 1894 as a residential hotel, though it later became a pub. With a frontage of 200ft and three floors, it offered family rooms and bachelors' chambers, with gardens and tennis courts at the back.

157. *The second Feathers Hotel* near Ealing Broadway Station c1910. The present pub was built in the 1920s.

158. *The Old Hats* in decayed condition in the 1890s.

159. *The Plough Inn, Little Ealing Lane c*1900.

160. *The Bell Inn* as refaced in the early 1900s.

161. *The Three Pigeons, High Street, Ealing* 1904. It was later rebuilt in grander style and obtained a full licence.

162. *The Park Hotel, Greenford Avenue, Hanwell* 1904. Part of the building was used as a theatre and cinema.

163. *Drayton Court Hotel in Ealing Illustrated,* 1894.

The Trams Issue

It was not until the end of the nineteenth century that railway companies in suburban Middlesex made a serious attempt to attract working class customers who, up till then, found neither the timetable convenient nor the fares within their income. After the Cheap Trains Act of 1883 obliged companies to provide cheap early morning fares for workmen, the GWR was the last of the metropolitan companies to do so. In an LCC enquiry in 1892 a police constable in Ealing reported that he had to call workmen as early as 3.30am to give them time to walk the four miles to Shepherds Bush, the nearest station from which they could get a workmen's train into London. The same was true for Hanwell, a further two miles out. As a concession the GWR scheduled one train leaving Southall at 5am, arriving at Paddington at 5.26am.

The cheap alternative was the tram. In 1876 the Southall, Ealing & Shepherds Bush Tram Railway Company began to operate a horse-drawn service between Shepherds Bush and Priory Road, Acton. However, it was more than twenty years before the route was extended west of Acton, which was not surprising because the tram company had financial

difficulties and the Ealing Local Board opposed the running of trams through Ealing anyway. The Board's opposition was echoed in May 1898 when Ealing Urban District Council protested against the plan of the London United Tramway Company (LUT), which then had possession of the old horse-tram route, to extend mechanised services through Ealing from Acton to Hanwell. This would, the Council objected, bring a mass of new people into the area and encourage jerry-building. Montague Nelson, chairman of the Council, argued that the changes would force out existing residents, many of whom had come to Ealing to escape trams elsewhere. Charles Jones, the Council surveyor, objected to the overhead wires. In evidence to the House of Commons committee it was said that 'the tramway brings a different element into the neighbourhood. The old order disappears and the character of the neighbourhood gradually changes.'

But the Council did not necessarily represent the public's view. The municipal elections of 1898 were fought largely on the issue of the trams and the anti-tram lobby were reduced to a majority of one. After about 18 months the inevitable was recognised and the opposition to trams collapsed. Ealing UDC gave notice in 1899 to the Board of Trade that it wished to build two tram links of its own, one across Ealing from Acton to Hanwell, the other from the Uxbridge Road along Longfield Avenue. A deal was struck with the LUT in 1900 by which the com-

164. The arrival of the trams. The procession of cars at Ealing Town Hall, where speeches were made, 10 July 1901.

165. *A London United Electric Tramways car* at West Ealing c1905, en route to Shepherd's Bush.

pany built its own tracks but paid Ealing Council compensation, and a £500 per annum wayleave. In addition it had to widen roads, pave the tramway in hard wood, and ensure that the standards carrying the wires were also capable of use for street lighting.

The LUT track to Southall was opened on 10 July 1901 with a grand procession of new cars. On the return trip there was a stop at Ealing Town Hall where Lord Rothschild made a speech. Another route between Brentford and Hanwell opened in 1906.

The competition of the trams had an effect on fares on other services. The LUT charge for Southall to Shepherds Bush return was 2d, and to the City and back, 4d. This forced down fares on the buses and the District Railway which, in 1901, made workmen's tickets available up to 7.30am.

In many ways the anxieties of the Ealing residents were borne out. In the early years there were complaints about the noise of the trams, and modifications were made to cars and track. As regards the feared influx of population and the threat of jerry building, in the decade following 1901 Ealing's population rose 85% to 61,222, and its housing stock by 101% to 12,599.

Although some of this building can be accounted for by infilling and the creation of Brentham Village (see p. 131), much of it was caused by low-cost housing concentrated in Northfields and South Ealing. LUT in a publicity book entitled *To Uxbridge from the City by tram, tube and car via Ealing or Harrow* put a gloss on the matter: 'Until recent years few new houses were built in Ealing of less rental than £70 or £80 a year, and a considerable portion of the area is occupied almost exclusively by houses with rents ranging from the figure mentioned to £200 a year and more. But in South and West Ealing cheaper houses from £70 to pretty semi-detached villas at £30 have been and are being built in response to public demand that shows little sign of abating. While the electric trams have not driven out the richer class of inhabitant from Ealing, they have made the borough a pleasant place of residence for those less well endowed with the world's goods.'

Hanwell's population increased by 83% to 19129 and its new housing stock, in the south and east, formed a continuous belt of building with the new districts of Ealing.

In the same period Ealing Council built its first municipal housing, or workmen's cottages as they were described, on a site near the junction of Pope's Lane and Ealing Road. From 1899 some 140 houses were built.

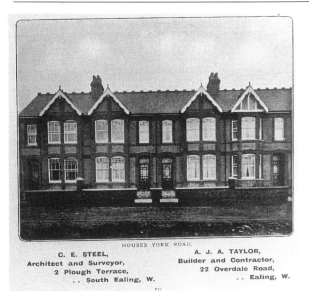

HOUSES YORK ROAD.

C. E. STEEL,	A. J. A. TAYLOR,
Architect and Surveyor,	Builder and Contractor,
2 Plough Terrace,	22 Overdale Road,
.. South Ealing, W.	.. Ealing, W.

166. Advertisement for new houses in South Ealing, from the *Ealing Official Guide* 1912.

A REALLY GOOD WELL-BUILT HOUSE

Of Unique Design, Extra Well Fitted, Charming Position, Gravel Soil, High and Healthy Situation, two minutes of South Ealing or Northfield Halt Stations on Metropolitan District Railway. 35 minutes City. 8 minutes Service. Season Ticket per quarter to Mansion House, £2.

Price, £250

CAN BE BOUGHT BY PAYING £10 DOWN, BALANCE AS RENT.

A MARVEL OF VALUE.

LARGE ROOMS.—Dining Room, Drawing Room, Three Bedrooms, Bathroom with Bath, Lavatory Basin, etc. Good Combined Kitchen. Nice Front Garden planted with Shrubs. Good Garden at Back. Tiled Forecourt and Lincrusta Dado to Hall. Special Economical Heating System.

Call and see Houses in

York Road and Bramley Road and Northfield Avenue, SOUTH EALING.

Also Houses of Rentals from 12/6 per week to £100 per year and from £250 to £1000 for Sale

THE SOUTH MARDER ESTATE OFFICE,

2 Plough Terrace, South Ealing.

167. Ealing's first council houses – Municipal Cottages, South Ealing, in 1903.

Co-Partnership in Housing.

WOODFIELD AVENUE, EALING, W.
(LOOKING NORTH),
From a Photograph by S. J. MUIR, September, 1905.

THESE HOUSES ARE THE FREEHOLD PROPERTY OF THE

Ealing Tenants, Limited.

A Society registered under the Industrial and Provident Societies' Acts,
and is known throughout the whole of the United Kingdom.

RENTS of HOUSES, from 10/6 per week (inclusive).

TO TENANTS AND INVESTORS, BEST RESULTS.

		Per Annum.
A GOOD	SHARE CAPITAL (limit £200) ...	5 per cent.
INVESTMENT.	LOAN STOCK (no limit)	4 per cent.

INSPECT THE ESTATE, OR WRITE FOR PARTICULARS,

To SECRETARY,
ESTATE OFFICE, WOODFIELD ROAD,
PITSHANGER,
EALING, W.

☞ At the Top of Eaton Rise.

168. Advertisement for Ealing Tenants Ltd., from the *Ealing and Hanwell Year Book* 1906.

169. The first Brentham houses under construction – Vivian Terrace, Woodfield Road.

The Brentham Experiment

Unconventional housing was developed at the extreme north of the district. This was the Brentham estate. Up to 1900 the area north of Mount Avenue was still largely farmland and Pitshanger Lane a track that led to Pitshanger farm.

The idea for Brentham village came from a long tradition of attempts to improve the housing of the working classes. Some philanthropic factory owners had built whole towns for their workforce, such as Saltaire or Port Sunlight. But there was also a tradition of self-help, typified by the formation of the building society movement. To these were added the garden city ideas of Ebenezer Howard, who believed that with the right stimulus people could improve their own conditions.

In 1891 Howard put his ideas into practice by forming a co-operative building firm, General Builders Ltd. One of its branches was in Ealing, and in 1897 six members of the firm decided to work together to buy plots of land in Woodfield Road, between Mount Avenue and Pitshanger Lane, and build nine houses. The £400 needed for the land was put up by Mr and Mrs Stobart Greenhalgh. The men involved met with the Liberal MP, Henry Vivian, who encouraged them to form a tenants' association; a company was formed which was registered in 1901 as Ealing Tenants Ltd. Such was the support for the venture that by September 1901 Henry Vivian could announce that nearly £1000 had been raised and that the first nine houses were nearing completion.

By 1905 fifty terraced houses had been put up in Woodfield Road, Crescent and Avenue and in Brunner Road. More land was bought from the Fowlers Hill estate and in 1907 another thirty acres added from Pitshanger Farm. With such a substantial development in prospect, the garden city planners, Raymond Unwin and Barry Parker, who were working in Hampstead Garden Suburb, were brought in. They arranged the houses in informal groups with generous gardens, offering a variety of perspectives.

All the houses were owned by Ealing Tenants Ltd and were let at rents ranging from 6s 6d to 21s per

week, and all had baths though not all had bath-
rooms. They compared favourably, however, with
other working-class housing of the time. Central to
the philosophy of the founders was that communal
facilities should be provided on the estate; land was
reserved for allotments and playing fields, and a
club, the Brentham Institute, was completed in
1911. Here, dances, whist drives, concerts and lec-
tures were held; flower shows and pageants, including a May-day celebration, were regular events.
Other amenities were scarce: there was only one
school at first, no church until the building of St
Barnabas in 1916, public transport was poor, and it
was a twenty minute walk to the Broadway.

In its early days Brentham Garden estate was surrounded by open land, but the building of Western
Avenue and the transformation of Hanger Lane into
part of the North Circular brought more speculative
building which changed the outlook and enclosed
the estate. Large-scale council housing reduced
working-class demand and Ealing Tenants began to
sell some of the houses and opened the club to non-
residents. This trend accelerated after World War II,
but the physical character of the village has been
retained and is now protected as a conservation
area.

171. *Meadvale Road and Holyoake Walk.*

170. *Ludlow Road.*

172. *Crowning the Brentham May Queen* 1921.

173. A meeting of Ealing Tenants Ltd, *c*1901.

Ealing Studios

Ealing Studios, famous for a string of comedy films in the 1940s, had their origin as early as 1904 when William George Barker, an established film producer, moved to Ealing. His choice was apparently determined by the clean environment, and the general absence of industry and fogs. He bought a house called West Lodge, set back from Ealing Green, and here set up Barker Motion Photography Ltd. By 1912 these studios were the largest in England, the three glasshouse-like stages built in the five-acre garden of the house. He made many spectacular films, including such epics as the *Battle of Waterloo*, *The Great Bullion Robbery* and *Jane Shore*, before retiring in 1918.

The studios were then rented out for a number of years, but in 1929 they were bought by Associated Radio Pictures, whose head of production was Basil Dean. Sound stages with the latest facilities were designed by Messrs Robert Atkinson, and the building known as the Lodge, which faced on to Ealing Green, was converted into an administration block.

Production started in late 1931 and Dean supervised a number of successful films with home-grown stars like Gracie Fields and George Formby. When Dean resigned in 1938 Michael Balcon took his place and the production company became known as Ealing Studios Ltd. The 1940s and early 1950s saw a series of distinguished films made here. The fine war films were succeeded by the famous Ealing comedies, including *Kind Hearts and Coronets* and *The Lavender Hill Mob*. In the mid–1950s, however, the British film industry was in recession and the studios were sold in 1955 to the BBC, who continue to use them for film production.

Despite its considerable size the studio complex makes little visual impact on Ealing Green, but the impressive bulk of the sound stages can be appreciated from Walpole Park. Their presence here has resulted in Ealing being used as a location quite frequently in television programmes, just as it once was in feature films.

174. *The Ealing Studios complex* in 1953. The entrance was beside the white building at the bottom of the picture, which faces on to Ealing Green. West Lodge is the white house on the right.

Filling in the Gaps

Although Ealing and Hanwell are seen as essentially Victorian creations, much of the housing was put up in the Edwardian era and after World War I. Undoubtedly the availability of better railway services played an important, though not decisive, part in stimulating new building, particularly in the north-east and north-west corners of Ealing. The Foundation Company built semi-detached houses on the Argyle Park Estate, selling from £800 to £1700, while detached houses went from £1850 to £2250. This estate occupies a site between Argyle Road and the railway and includes Vallis Way, Fosse Way, Bruton Way, Avalon Road and Crossway. Further east the Wimpey Company built semi-detached houses valued between £1450 and £1590 in Kent Avenue. There was also much infilling of existing streets: for example, some plots in Castlebar Park Road, a road originally laid out in the 1870s, were only built on in the 1920s.

In Hanwell part of the Hanwell Park Estate had been built before 1914, from Greenford Avenue towards the railway line. The remaining north-west corner, towards Greenford and the River Brent, known as Elthorne Heights, was completed in 1935. The closure in 1933 of the Central London District School released a large amount of land and on this the LCC built the Cuckoo estate, with some 1592 houses completed by 1939, laid out in a style influenced by the garden city movement. Part of the old school buildings were retained and the tree-lined drive that led to the school was incorporated into the road layout as Cuckoo Avenue.

The last railway line into Ealing was the Ealing & Shepherds Bush, promoted by the GWR to connect with the West London Railway. Construction began in 1912, but work was slow, and it was not until August 1920 that it was open to the public. Platforms were inserted between the lines of the District and the GWR main line at Ealing Broadway, and a station was opened at West Acton. Ealing now enjoyed a city route speedier than either the District or the Great Western.

175. *Ealing Broadway Station* c1920, after the opening of the Central London Railway (later Central Line) service.

MODEL "R."
PRICE ONLY £800 FREEHOLD   DEPOSIT £80
Balance about 26/9 per week.
A larger deposit would mean a smaller weekly payment.
PRICE INCLUDES ROAD CHARGES AND FREE CONVEYANCE.

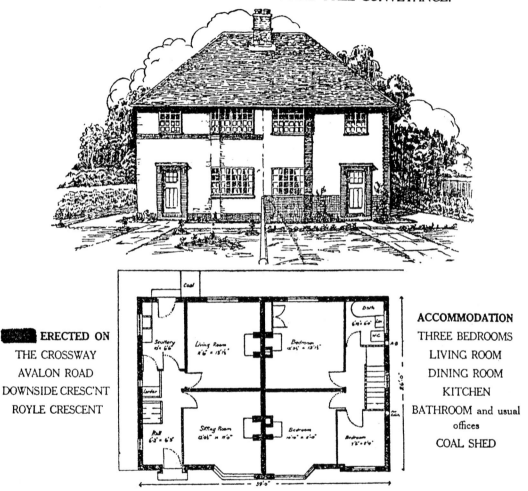

ERECTED ON

THE CROSSWAY
AVALON ROAD
DOWNSIDE CRESC'NT
ROYLE CRESCENT

ACCOMMODATION

THREE BEDROOMS
LIVING ROOM
DINING ROOM
KITCHEN
BATHROOM and usual
offices
COAL SHED

SPECIFICATION.

Hot and Cold Water will be supplied to Bath from Sitting Room Grate.   Two Gas Fires will be fitted in Bedrooms. Gas Copper fitted in Kitchen. Deep Pantry Sink, with tiles over. Shelves.

BACK BEDROOM. Cupboard.

The House will be Painted and Papered or Distempered to shades selected by purchasers. Wood Posts and Chains, with Wood Entrance Gate, and "Peerless" Wire Fencing at sides and rear. Electric Lamp holders. Ceiling Roses and Switches provided.

176. Developer's brochure for the Argyle Park estate, 1920s.

Entrance Front.

HOUSE AT EALING, MIDDLESEX

Welch and Lander, FF.R.I.B.A., Architects

GENERAL PARTICULARS: This is one of the Haymills houses on the Hanger Hill estate. It is a modern treatment of the four-bedroom house, with a sun-room on the roof.

CONSTRUCTION: External walls of 9-in. brickwork, with two coats of cement rendering, rubbed smooth with a wooden float and then given two coats of cream-coloured limewash. Flat roof of timber construction covered with three-ply waterproof roofing ("Macflex") protected by a ¾-in. thickness of specially prepared tarmacadam. Windows, standard metal casements, those in the sun-room being strengthened with hollow tubular mullions.

BUILDING COST: This house was built in 1934 by Haymills, Ltd., who state that a fair price for building a similar house on a reasonable site, with all services available, would be £1,400–£1,450.

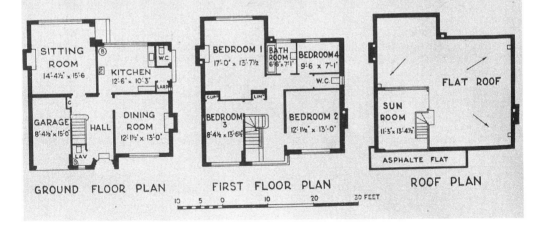

177. *House on the Haymills Estate, Hanger Hill.*

When the Wood properties were sold to the Prudential Assurance in 1906 the area east of Hanger Lane was still undeveloped. Hanger Hill House and its grounds had been let in 1901 as a golf course which operated until 1930. But in 1927 the Wood estate sold their land west of the Acton boundary to Haymills Ltd, having already sold the adjacent land in Acton to the Hanger Hill Garden Estate Ealing Ltd in 1925. The first houses in Audley Road were built in 1928 and the Haymills estate, mainly of modernist detached houses with four or five bedrooms and selling from £1475 to £1975, was mostly complete in 1939. Shops were built on the corner of Western Avenue and Hanger Lane and a cinema, originally known as the Ritz, in 1938.

Ealing Village, an estate of 128 flats in four-storey blocks, is notable for its Art Deco styling. It was built in the 1920s to the designs of R. Toms & Partners, on a thin strip of land between Madeley Road and the District Railway, with access from Hanger Lane.

During the 1939–45 war both Ealing and Hanwell, although not major targets, suffered some bomb damage. There has been much rebuilding since. Many of the large Victorian houses have been converted into flats and others, notably those in Kent Gardens, were demolished to make way for estates of smaller houses or flats. But there have been concerted attempts in recent years to prevent the further erosion of the character of Ealing's Victorian residential streets especially from the threat of backland development. House prices remain amongst the highest in London.

At the same time Ealing has changed from an exclusively residential suburb to a major commercial centre, with the replacement of houses along the Uxbridge Road by offices.

Hanwell has fared less well, somewhat overshadowed by its dominant neighbour whose shopping centre makes it difficult for Hanwell's shops to prosper, but the area near the church retains its charm and there are many pleasant residential streets.

The Ealing Broadway shopping area has been drastically altered in developments that swept away many of the back streets, and removed landmarks like Bentall's store. The new Ealing Broadway Centre provides offices, shops and a large public library and draws many people into the area. Ealing may no longer be 'Queen of the Suburbs' in quite the way it once was, but a prosperous future seems assured.

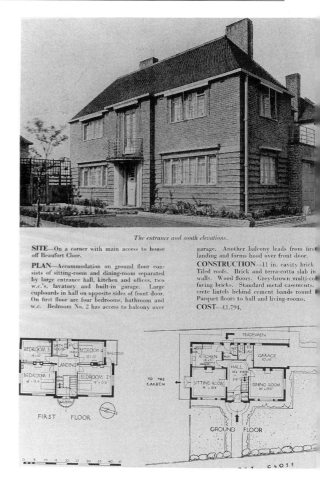

The entrance and south elevations.

SITE—On a corner with main access to house off Beaufort Close.

PLAN—Accommodation on ground floor consists of sitting-room and dining-room separated by large entrance hall, kitchen and offices, two w.c.'s, lavatory and built-in garage. Large cupboards in hall on opposite sides of front door. On first floor are four bedrooms, bathroom and w.c. Bedroom No. 2 has access to balcony over garage. Another balcony leads from first landing and forms hood over front door.

CONSTRUCTION—11 in. cavity brick. Tiled roofs. Brick and terra-cotta slab in walls. Wood floors. Grey-brown multi-col facing bricks. Standard metal casements, crete lintels behind cement bands round Parquet floors to hall and living-rooms.

COST—£1,794.

178. *House on the Haymills Estate, Hanger Hill.*

INDEX

Numbers in bold type refer to illustrations.